Flying Star Feng Shui Made Easy

Flying Star Feng Shui Made Easy

Third Edition

David Twicken

Writers Club Press
New York   Lincoln   Shanghai

Flying Star Feng Shui Made Easy
Third Edition

Writers Club Press
an imprint of iUniverse, Inc.

For information address:
iUniverse
2021 Pine Lake Road, Suite 100
Lincoln, NE 68512
www.iuniverse.com

ISBN: 0-595-09966-1

Printed in the United States of America

Disclaimer

The information in this book is based on the author's knowledge and personal experience. It is presented for educational purposes to assist the reader in expanding his or her knowledge of Asian philosophy and arts. The techniques and practices are to be used at the reader's own discretion and liability. The author is not responsible in any manner whatsoever for any physical injury or damage to property that may occur by following instructions in this book.

About this book

This book has been designed as a manual for applying Flying Stars Feng Shui in modern living spaces. I have presented the material in a format that focuses on prioritizing methods and remedies based on importance, relevance and practicality. This book offers a method to quickly apply Flying Stars Feng Shui in your home or office. Powerful non-Flying Stars Feng Shui methods, previously considered secret, are included in this book along with the Flying Stars methods, the combination offers a practical and potent system of Feng Shui that transcends the limitations of applying Flying Stars Feng Shui in modern living environments.

In the appendix you'll find Flying Stars charts for all of the twenty-year cycles. Each is labeled with key information about the chart, for instance, locked charts for Cycle Eight, Parent String, Pearl String or Double Stars meeting in Facing Palace.

There is material in this book that has never been published in English, ones which have been considered "Feng Shui Secrets," made available to only a select few. However, I consider them so valuable to the effective implementation of Feng Shui that I feel they must be made available to all practitioners. They are revealed here in a user-friendly way, not in the traditional method of deep metaphor that is impossible to comprehend for those not trained in these arts and in the Chinese language.

I hope you enjoy learning this magnificent metaphysical art and science. May it bring Health, Happiness and Prosperity to you and all you touch.

To contact the author, go to:
www.HealingQi.com

Contents

Introduction

In an ancient time, men and women lived close to nature and were able to perceive the subtle influences of physical, mental and spiritual aspects of life. In these deep states of awareness they recognized three major influences on the destiny of a person: Heaven, Humanity and Earth, the Three Treasures. Heaven's influences are revealed in Astrology and are a blueprint of one's life; Human Influences include one's actions, deeds and personal cultivation, and Earth influences are the effects of the environment. These three aspects of life are integrated, influencing each other throughout a lifetime. The following is an introduction to each of the three Taoist Arts.

Heaven's Influence-Chinese Astrology

Four Pillars of Destiny, also referred to as Zi Ping, Ba Zi or Five-Element Chinese Astrology, is the predominant astrology practiced in Asia. Four Pillars reveals Heaven's Influence on Destiny and Luck and shows the probable life path, including personality, character, health, marriage, wealth and career, and is a map for knowing the optimal time to pursue opportunities. Its highest use is assisting people in creating a happy, healthy and spiritually-positive life. Human Influences/Spiritual Qi Gong and Earth Influences/Feng Shui can transform Heaven's Influence.

Earth's Influence-Feng Shui

Feng Shui is the ancient art of harmonizing human life with one's environment. This natural art includes perceiving the influences of land forms, time, geographical direction and interior design in a home, office or any other living space. Feng Shui offers methods to generate prosperity, positive relationships, good health and personal development. There are many styles and forms of Feng Shui—this book contains proven methods that are easy to understand and apply, ones that are practiced by professionals around the world. Feng Shui is Earth Luck and can transform the effects of Heaven and Human Influences.

Human's Influence-Spiritual Qi Gong

Qi Gong means energy exercises or energy cultivation. It is an ancient practice of cultivating energy, or Qi, for health, vitality and, if one chooses, spiritual development. There are hundreds of styles and forms of Qi Gong. On a basic level, they are gentle types of breathing and movements that harmonize emotions and generate vitality. Qi Gong can also become Spiritual Qi Gong, which consists of specific meditations to assist a person in revealing and experiencing his or her true spiritual nature. This human cultivation transforms Heaven and Earth Influences.

Principles of Asian Philosophy

Qi

The ancients' view was that the Universe is filled with energy, an energy that moves through endless flows of transformation. This energy comprises all of life, including stars, planets, trees, mountains, water, animals and human life, and is called Qi. It includes both matter and energy, and it is also the force that allows the transformation from energy to matter and matter to energy. For example, water is a type of Qi and is a perfect example of how Qi transforms. Water can exist in the form of ice, ice can transform into water and water into steam. Qi is ice, Qi is water, Qi is steam and Qi is the heat that allows the transformation to occur. Qi is all of life. It takes form to become the densest substances and is also contained in the subtlest of substances. Every part of the Universe is a blend of different types of Qi. To understand this blending is to understand the energies of life. Knowing the rhythms and expressions of Qi is to be able to predict and transform life.

All tools used in the Asian arts are variations of Qi. This book introduces Yin-Yang, the Eight Trigrams, the Five-Element system and cycles of time. They are all different aspects or transformations of Qi, and help to calculate the effects of Qi on a person throughout his or her lifetime.

Yin-Yang

From the beginning of time, humanity has sought to understand Heaven, Earth and Human life, whether it be ancient Hindus in India, Aztecs in Mexico, Jews of Israel or the ancient Egyptians. In China, a model of understanding nature evolved which would form the roots of Chinese Philosophy, Acupuncture, Herbal Medicine, Qi Gong, Nutrition, Martial Arts, Feng Shui and Astrology. This system is Yin-Yang. Its theory includes viewing the Universe as one integrated whole, as well as two opposing but interdependent aspects. All aspects of life can be categorized into Yin-Yang, for example, Heaven-Earth, man-woman, hot-cold, left-right, light-dark, front-back, hard-soft, north-south, east-west, root-branch, top-bottom, fast-slow, waxing-waning, timely-untimely, empty-full and auspicious-inauspicious. Yin-Yang theory categorizes any situation into two parts. Each part gives life to its opposite—there must be a left to have right, a strong to have weak, a front to have back—they are not two separate entities, but two sides of the same situation; they give life to each other and never separate. Yin-Yang is a model which views a situation as consisting of two parts while simultaneously existing as one inseparable whole. This dynamic is integral to understanding Yin-Yang.

Yin-Yang is a predominant component in Asian art. One major application of Yin-Yang theory is Yang representing a growing or expanding phase and Yin a declining phase. All of life flows through this basic model of rising and declining. Each expansion leads to a decline, leading to another expansion and decline in an endless cycle. This universal reality is the basis for this book and for Flying Stars Feng Shui.

Five Elements

Five Elements, or Wu Xing, is the basis of most Chinese Metaphysics. They are the ABCs of calculating, evaluating and applying the knowledge of Feng Shui. The following explains the Five Elements.

A circle can be viewed as one integrated whole.

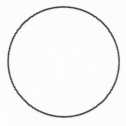

This same circle can be viewed in two aspects, Yin and Yang.

Top
Yang

Bottom
Yin

A circle can be viewed as consisting of five segments or phases, the Five Elements/Phases.

Five Elements/Phases

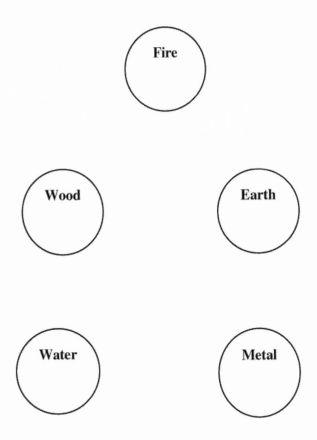

Each circle or phase is assigned an element: water, wood, fire, earth and metal. Each element maintains a position within the circle. For example, wood is positioned where the circle begins to move upward and represents growth, or Spring; fire is located where the portion of the circle reaches its peak, symbolizing Summer; earth is positioned where harvesting takes place, representing Indian Summer; metal represents turning inward or contraction, representing Autumn; and water is where the circle turns completely inward to regenerate, representing Winter. Water also reflects preparation for a new Spring, wood or growth cycle. This cycle continues infinitely and reflects self-generation and the eternal nature of life.

The relative position of each of the Five Elements or Five Phases in the circle determines its specific relationship with every other element. For example, water is mother to wood, grandparent to fire, grandchild of earth and child of metal. Each element has similarly distinct relationships with the four remaining elements. The ability to apply those relationships is a key to learning and applying the Asian arts. The chart below summarizes these relationships.

Five-Element Relationships

Element ➔	Water	Wood	Fire	Earth	Metal
Parent	Metal	Water	Wood	Fire	Earth
Sibling, Same	Water	Wood	Fire	Earth	Metal
Child, Offspring	Wood	Fire	Earth	Metal	Water
Grandchild	Fire	Earth	Metal	Water	Wood
Grandparent, Controller	Earth	Metal	Water	Wood	Fire

Interpreting This Chart

Water's parent is metal
Water's sibling is water
Water's child is wood
Water's grandchild is fire
Water's controller is earth

From these five relationships we see five key interactions.

1. Each element gives to another element, the parent.
2. Each element controls another element, the grandparent or controller.
3. Each element is controlled by another element, the grandchild.
4. Each element receives from another element, the child.
5. Each element is supported by another element, the same element, or sibling.

These relationships are expressed in the actions of giving, receiving, controlling and being controlled. Living a natural, healthy life depends on finding balance within these five interactions. One action is not better than another; there is only meaning when compared to a given situation. Some situations need nourishment, others control, and still others need to give; what is beneficial is relative to the condition of all elements. These Five-Elements are applied in unique ways in Feng Shui and other Chinese Metaphysics.

The following chart summarizes these relationships.

Situation	First Action
Weakness	Nourish 1. Add same or sibling element 2. Add the parent element
Too Strong or Excessive	1. Add the child

The following diagrams illustrate how each element is affected by all elements. Familiarize yourself with these relationships—they are integral in the application of Chinese Metaphysics. Practice selecting which elements are needed in conditions of excessiveness or deficiency.

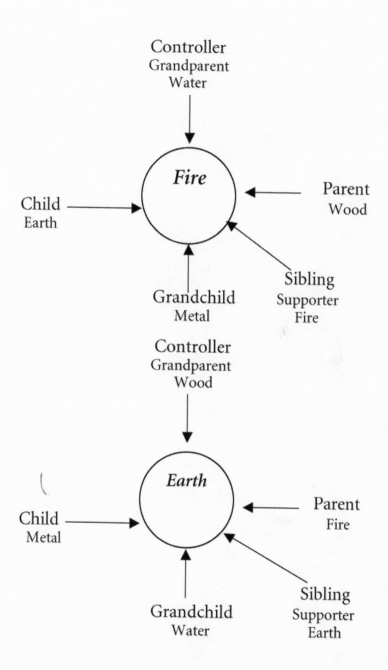

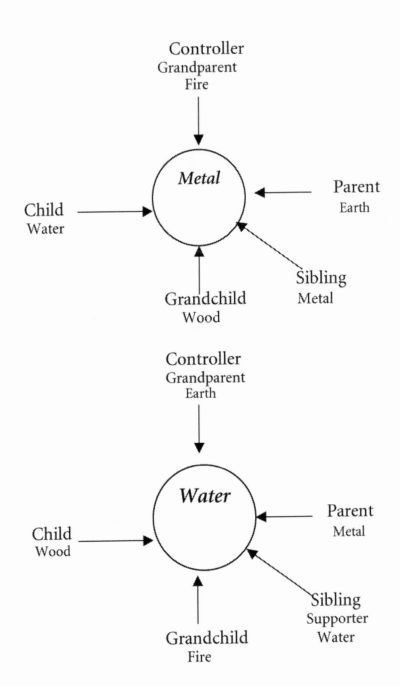

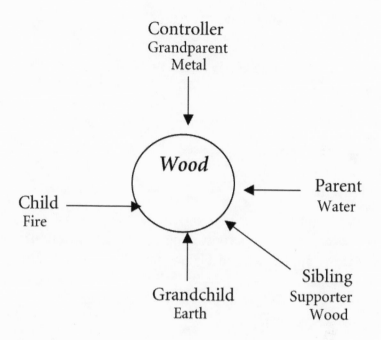

Five-Element Corrections

Element	Corrections for Excess	Corrections for Weakness
Water	Wood	Water, Metal
Wood	Fire	Wood, Water
Fire	Earth	Fire, Wood
Earth	Metal	Earth, Fire
Metal	Water	Metal, Earth

Five-Element Cycles

The Five Elements interact in a variety of ways, or cycles. The three major cycles are promotion, controlling and reduction and they are the basis for many applications in Flying Stars Feng Shui. The following diagrams explain each cycle.

Promotion Cycle

The promotion cycle is the parent-to-child relationship. It is a cycle that nourishes, supplements or strengthens its child element. Its influence can be favorable or unfavorable depending on the condition of the elements. The following diagram illustrates the promotion cycle.

Promotion Cycle

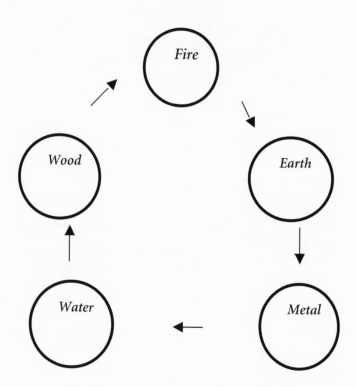

Promotion Cycle

1. Water placed on wood promotes growth—water is the mother of wood.
2. Wood placed in fire promotes growth—wood is the mother of fire.
3. Fire transforms substances into ashes or earth—fire is the mother of earth.
4. Metal is found within earth—earth is the mother of metal.
5. Metal can be liquefied into water—metal is the mother of water.

Controlling Cycle

The controlling cycle is the grandparent-to-grandchild relationship, or the controlling cycle. Its influence can be favorable or unfavorable depending on the conditions of the elements. The following diagram illustrates the controlling cycle.

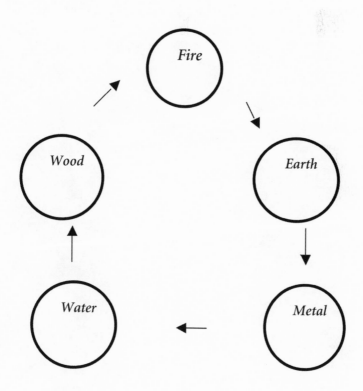

Controlling Cycle

1. Fire melts metal or controls metal—grandparent relationship.
2. Metal cuts wood or controls wood—grandparent relationship.
3. Wood absorbs nutrients from the earth and controls earth—grandparent relationship.
4. Earth absorbs water or controls water—grandparent relationship.
5. Water puts out fire or controls fire—grandparent relationship.

Reduction Cycle

The controlling cycle controls, dominates or weakens and when it over-acts; when it is too strong it creates an imbalance. The reduction cycle is used to harmonize this condition. The promotion and reduction cycles are arranged identically, the only difference being the flow of energy—the promotional cycle flows clockwise and the reduction cycle flows counter-clockwise.

Reduction Cycle

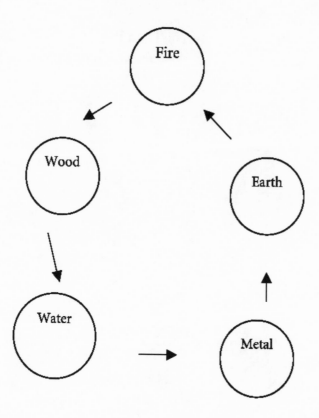

Reduction Cycle
1. Water is the child of metal—water takes from metal, reducing its influence.
2. Metal is the child of earth—metal takes from earth, reducing its influence.
3. Earth is the child of fire—earth takes from fire, reducing its influence.
4. Fire is the child of wood—fire takes from wood, reducing its influence.
5. Wood is the child of water—wood takes from water, reducing its influence.

The parent wants to give to the child and the child wants to take from the parent. This dynamic results in a decrease in the potency or magnitude of the parent.

Flying Stars Feng Shui

Introduction to Flying Stars Feng Shui

Feng Shui is the art and science of living in harmony with one's environment. It consists of principles and methods from Chinese philosophy, metaphysics, divination, science and experimentation. These natural principles are used to evaluate how nature influences health, marriage, emotions, finances, career, wealth, creativity, fertility and happiness. As with most ancient Chinese Metaphysics, Feng Shui's roots can be found in the *I Ching/Book of Changes,* which describes how the Universe functions. A profound concept in the *I Ching* is that life is always changing, and that to obtain happiness one needs to learn to live in harmony with change. Flying Stars Feng Shui is about change. It teaches how to evaluate the changing influences of nature and offers ways to optimize favorable and minimize unfavorable influences.

Flying Stars Feng Shui is a natural and dynamic form of Feng Shui and is the most common form practiced by professional Feng Shui consultants throughout Asia. The advanced levels of this system have been a closely guarded secret and are seldom clearly explained. Environmental forms, interior design, time and direction comprise the major aspects of Flying Stars Feng Shui. Flying Stars is comparable to a CAT scan or an MRI— these medical diagnostics capture the deepest aspects hidden to the human eye. Flying Stars Feng Shui captures both visible and hidden influences affecting living environments. It is capable of perceiving influences that other systems of Feng Shui are incapable of perceiving, making it a powerful tool for transformation.

Background

Feng Shui has evolved over thousands of years, revealing nature's influences on all aspects of life. This body of knowledge has been passed from generation to generation and is called "Kan Yu" Feng Shui. Feng means "Wind" and Shui means "Water." Kan means "The Way of Heaven," or the influences of time, and Yu means "The Way of Earth." Kan Yu is the study of how time (Heaven) influences living environments (earth). Feng Shui began with the Forms School, which evaluates the landscape, and evolved to include Qi formulas that evaluate the effects of time and space/direction. Traditional Feng Shui evolved to include forms, time and space.

Modern traditional Feng Shui has four major branches. The following summarizes these systems.

1. Classical San Yuan has two major styles:
    a). Primordial San Yuan (three cycles), believed to be developed by Yang, Yun Son, in the Tang Dynasty (618–906 CE). This system uses a compass with the sixty-four hexagrams of the *I Ching*, the Nine Stars and stems and branches to determine the most auspicious directions of a building. It was primarily used for Yin Feng Shui, or the selection and placement of gravesites, emphasizing Land or Forms Feng Shui.

    b). San Yuan Xuan Kong is the next stage of evolution of San Yuan and focuses on Yang Feng Shui, or the buildings where people live. This system uses the Nine Palaces, time, mountain, water, annual and monthly Flying Stars, environmental forms, interior design, Five-Element remedies and cycles of time. It integrates land forms and the Flying Stars of a building.

2.   Classical Xuan Kong

This system uses Flying Stars, the Nine Palaces and special star conditions and emphasizes Construction Star and Water Star interactions. Environmental forms are not emphasized. This system was founded by Hsu, Jen Wang, during the Song Dynasty (960–1279). This system was designed for buildings, enhancing Primordial San Yuan to include forms and Qi in a building. The application and meanings of stars can differ from San Yuan Feng Shui.

3.   San Ho

This style uses a special compass, San Ho Luo Pan. It emphasizes stems, branches and the Nine Stars in selecting proper sites and auspicious facing positions. This system focuses on Mountain Qi (Dragon Veins) and Water Qi (Water Dragons). It is believed that Yang, Yun Son, founded this system.

In my experience, current professionals combine the best of these classical Feng Shui styles. The material in this book presents both basic and advanced aspects of these traditional forms of Feng Shui and is applicable for most modern-day living environments.

The origins of Feng Shui are found in an ancient time, beginning with the discovery of the Eight Trigrams by the legendary Fu Xi; this lead to King Wen creating the I Ching in the Zhou Dynasty. These two men are associated with the Early and Later Heaven Ba Guas, the foundation of Flying Stars Feng Shui.

Tracing Feng Shui through history reveals the following pioneers of Classical Feng Shui. The following people are those publicly known for their contributions, but there are most likely others who contributed to the development of this ancient art.

Ching Wu
Han Dynasty
Wu wrote *The Burial* and is a pioneer of Kan Yu Feng Shui. He was influential in the development of the Forms Schools.

Guo Po
Jin Dynasty
Guo Po wrote the classic *Treatise of Burial*, which contains many of the principles of traditional Feng Shui.

Yang Yun Son
Tang Dynasty
Yang was the dominant Feng Shui Master in the Tang and Sung Dynasties. Yang founded the San Yuan (Three Cycles or Periods) and San Ho (Three Combinations) systems of Feng Shui. Emphasis was on the energy and influence of mountains and land forms. Yang, known as "Yang, Helper of the Poor," was best known for revealing that valleys have an influential Qi and exert as important an influence as mountains.

Hsu Jen Wang
Song Dynasty
Hsu transformed the San Yuan School, incorporating Flying Stars and their influence in buildings, and is considered the father of Xuan Kong Feng Shui. This style of Feng Shui includes land, forms and Flying Stars and is especially applicable for modern society, which does not have the same land forms as ancient ones.

Jiang Da Hong
Ming Dynasty
Jiang lived in the Ming and Qing Dynasties and is considered the first to write publicly about Xuan Kong/Flying Stars Feng Shui. He wrote in deep metaphorical language whose true meaning would be virtually impossible to understand without training. Jiang Da Hong is one of the most famous of all Feng Shui masters.

Zhang Zhung Shan
Qing Dynasty
Zhang lived during the last years of the Qing Dynasty and is credited for producing written texts clarifying Jiang's work.

Shen Ju Reng
Qing Dynasty Shen
Shen is responsible for organizing and clearly explaining Flying Stars Feng Shui, particularly Jiang's and Zhang's work. He is known for revealing information clearly to those that desired to learn, unlike his predecessors, who kept most of this information secret. It is very interesting to note that Shen never studied under a teacher—he learned through books. Shen lived during the end of the Qing Dynasty, and his son published *Shen's Xuan Kong Feng Shui*.

Flying Stars Feng Shui's effectiveness and power resides in its consideration of time and space. The combination of time and space creates an energy field in a building—direction is constant while time changes and each new cycle brings new, energetic influences that affect health, wealth, finances, romance, creativity and performance. In addition to time and direction, environment, forms, interior design, architecture and personal energy are also key aspects of Flying Stars Feng Shui.

A major form of Feng Shui is *San Yuan,* which means Three Cycles, and is the basis of Flying Stars Feng Shui. San Yuan consists of three cycles of twenty years, comprising one great cycle of sixty. This cycle of sixty is part of a greater cycle of one hundred and eighty.

Cycle	Cycle	Years
Upper	1	1864-1883
	2	1884-1903
	3	1904-1923
Middle	4	1924-1943
	5	1944-1963
	6	1964-1983
Lower	7	1984-2003
	8	2004-2023
	9	2024-2043

The essence of Flying Stars is that a particular Qi is prevalent during each twenty-year cycle. This Qi is the related period number, or Star Qi. For example, during 2004–2023, the predominant, Wang or timely Qi is the number eight. These twenty-year cycles are based on the cycles of planets Jupiter (wood) and Saturn (earth). Approximately every twenty years, these two planets align, causing a major energy shift that plays an integral role in Flying Stars Feng Shui.

Feng Shui's Yin-Yang, Qi and Five-Elements

Yin-Yang is a predominant component in Feng Shui. One major principle of the Yin-Yang theory is that Yang represents a growing, or expanding, phase and Yin a declining phase. All of life follows this basic model of rising and declining—each expansion leads to a decline, leading to another expansion and decline, in an endless cycle. In Flying Stars Feng Shui, energies, or stars, move through phases of favorable (Yang) and unfavorable (Yin) cycles.

Qi has many meanings, including air, energy, life force, spirit, matter and any other influence in life.

In Feng Shui there are two major applications:

1.   Sheng Qi includes favorable or positive influences of Qi.
2.   Sha Qi includes unfavorable or negative influences of Qi.

In traditional Feng Shui, the terms Sha Qi and Sheng Qi are commonly used. For example, a building can be a Sha Qi, a negative influence, or a lake in front of a house can be Sheng Qi, a positive influence.

Every element of the Universe, including stars, planets, lakes, oceans, mountains, people, etc., is made of Qi and has a particular influence in life. Evaluating the effects of Qi on the human body is the profession of acupuncturists. Evaluating the influences in living environments is the job of Feng Shui consultants. The tools each uses are slightly different, but the principles are the same.

One way to view life is that everything is a blend of Qi. If we can learn how to manage Qi, we learn how to manage life. Feng Shui is about managing Qi. We first learn to diagnose a Qi condition and then manage it by optimizing opportunities and reducing negative influences. Yin-Yang and the Five Elements are the key tools used in diagnosis and treatment.

Five-Elements

There are three cycles used in Flying Stars Feng Shui:

1. Promoting—Creation—Nourishing—Parent—Sheng Cycle
2. Controlling—Dominating—Grandparent—Ko Cycle
3. Reduction—Sedation—Child Cycle

The following are general rules for applying the Five Elements:

1. When two favorable elements in the promotion cycle interact, no correction is necessary.

    Examples:

    1. Water and Wood
    2. Wood and Fire
    3. Fire and Wood
    4. Earth and Metal
    5. Metal and Earth

2. When elements in the controlling cycle interact, the ideal method of correction is the reduction cycle.

    Method:

    Identify the element that is the controller. Add the child element of this controller to reduce its influence.

    Example 1

    Metal and Wood
    Metal controls wood and water is the child of metal. Water takes energy from metal, directing metal's energy away from wood.

The proper correction is adding water. Water is also the parent of wood and strengthens it.

Example 2

Water and Fire
Water controls fire and Water produces wood, therefore wood is the child of water. Add wood to this combination to break the domination and achieve harmony.

Basically, there are three situations in Flying Stars:

1. A promotion cycle interaction, for example, water and wood or fire and earth.
2. A controlling cycle interaction, for example, fire and metal or earth and water.
3. A same element interaction, for example, water and water or fire and fire.

If two of the same elements interact and they are favorable, the following can be applied:

1. Add the same element to reinforce it.
2. Add the parent element to strengthen it.

If two of the same elements interact and they are unfavorable, it is best to do the following:

1. Add the child element. For example, if two negative earths exist, add metal—it reduces the influence of negative earth.

These principles are the key to learning Flying Stars Feng Shui.

Eight Trigrams—Ba Gua

The Universe can be viewed in a macro or micro way. Evaluating the Universe in a micro way involves categorizing the Universe into smaller parts. Yin-Yang views the whole in two parts, Five Elements views the whole in five parts and the Eight Trigrams views the whole in eight parts; each system provides a different and unique method to perceive, understand and manage Universal influences.

The ancient book *I Ching* begins with Yin-Yang and expands into the Eight Trigrams. The following diagram illustrates this process. Each Trigram has three lines. For Feng Shui purposes, the top line represents the sky, the middle line a building and the bottom line the landscape.

_____   Sky or Stars
_____   Building
_____   Landscape

A trigram, or gua, reflects the concept of integration whereby each line influences the other two lines. Evaluating all lines is required to obtain a complete understanding of a situation—sky/stars, building and landscape must all be evaluated. Each trigram is a code that has a variety of related information that is the foundation for Flying Stars Feng Shui.

A circle represents the oneness of life—out of this oneness we can view
life in two major parts, Yin and Yang. Yin-Yang can expand in many ways.
One is the trinity of life: Heaven, Human and Earth, which is reflected by
the three-line gua, or trigram. Each of the three lines can be combined in
eight ways, the Eight Trigrams or Guas. These guas are a major aspect of
Flying Stars Feng Shui. They are a code that reveals information about
influences of nature in a building and their effect on its residents.

Yang   Yin

A classical representation

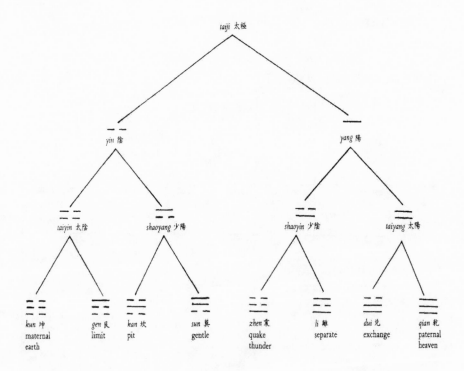

The following table contains basic information about each gua. The information is used to evaluate influences in a building.

Eight Trigram Corresponds

Trigram	Name	Number	Element	Color	Location	Family	Disease
— — ——— — —	Kan	1	Water	Blue Black	North	Second Son	Kidneys, Ears, Blood
— — — — — —	Kun	2	Earth	Yellow Beige	South West	Mother, Elderly Women	Stomach, Spleen, Abdomen, Digestion
— — — — ———	Zhen	3	Wood Thunder	Green	East	Eldest Son	Feet, Lungs, Throat
——— ——— — —	Xun	4	Wood Wind	Green	South East	Eldest Daughter	Buttocks, Thighs, Colds
		5	Earth		Center		Spleen, Stomach, Digestion, All kinds of illness
——— ——— ———	Qian	6	Metal Heaven	White Gold	North West	Father, Elderly Male	Head, Lungs, Mouth
— — ——— ———	Dui	7	Metal Lake	White Gold	West	Youngest Daughter	Pulmonary Disease, Headaches
——— — — — —	Gen	8	Earth Mountain	Yellow Beige	North East	Youngest Male	Hands, Fingers, Back
——— — — ———	Li	9	Fire	Red Purple	South	Second Daughter	Heart, Eyes

Ba Gua

The practice of Feng Shui began in an ancient time (estimated 3000 BCE) with the legendary Fu Xi, who revealed the Early Heaven Ba Gua arrangement of the Eight Trigrams.

Fu Xi's Ba Gua, Early Heaven Arrangement, Xian Tian Ba Gua

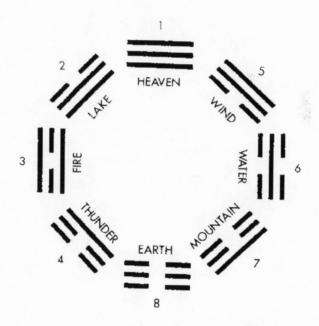

- Heaven is above and Earth below—they are in opposite positions.

- Thunder is the eldest son and Wind the eldest daughter—they are in opposite positions.
- Mountain is the youngest son and Lake is the youngest daughter—they are in opposite positions.
- Water is the middle son and fire the middle daughter—they are in opposite positions.
- This arrangement represents the transformation from Yang to Yin in a clockwise flow—they are in opposite positions.
- The sum of the gua lines or strokes for each opposite pair is nine, for example, earth is six lines and heaven in three lines, adding up to nine.

Wen Wang, the founder of the Zhou Dynasty, revealed a variation of the Ba Gua called the "Later Heaven Arrangement." This arrangement is based on the Five Elements, the eight geographical directions and, eventually, the Luo Shu Nine Stars.

Wen Wang Ba Gua, Later Heaven Arrangement, Hou Tian Ba Gua

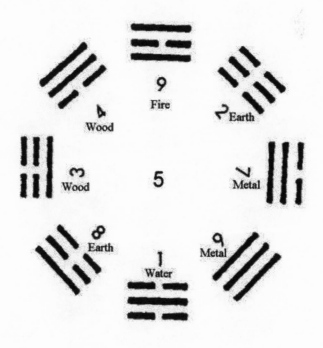

Nine Palaces

Luo Shu Magic Square

The Nine-Palace method is used to create Flying Star charts. The later Heaven Ba Gua is placed onto the Luo Shu to create the original pattern. The following Nine-Palace pattern reflects the original positions of the guas.

Nine-Palace Magic Square

Later Heaven Arrangement

Xun 4	Li 9	Kun 2
Zhen 3	5	Dui 7
Gen 8	Kan 1	Qian 6

This magic square has many applications. If we add opposite numbers diagonally and horizontally, they equal fifteen, reflecting balance. If we eliminate the five in the center palace, all the numbers add up to ten.

This is a significant Flying Stars chart formation and will be explained later in the book.

This Nine-Palace matrix will be the basis for the creation of all charts. The guas and numbers in each palace are the original positions of the guas, but more guas or stars will enter each palace based on two components, time and direction.

Below are the Eight Trigrams arranged in the Nine Palaces in Early Heaven, Later Heaven and combined patterns. All three applications are used in Flying Stars Feng Shui.

Early Heaven Ba Gua

Dui 7	*Qian* 6	*Xun* 4
Li 9		*Kan* 1
Zhen 3	*Kun* 2	*Gen* 8

Later Heaven Ba Gua

☴ Xun 4	☲ Li 9	☷ Kun 2
☳ Zhen 3	5	☱ Dui 7
☶ Gen 8	☵ Kan 1	☰ Qian 6

Early and Later Heaven Ba Gua

South East 7 Dui	South 6 Qian	South West 4 Xun
4 Xun	9 Li	2 Kun
East 9 Li		West 1 Kan
3 Zhen		7 Dui
North East 3 Zhen	North 2 Kun	North West 8 Gen
8 Gen	1 Kan	6 Qian

Early Heaven Gua is the top row.

Later Heaven Gua is the bottom row.

Luo Pan—Compass

A Luo Pan is a Chinese Feng Shui compass. It is a basic compass with a variety of Feng Shui information, including the Eight Trigrams, the Five Elements, the eight cardinal geographical locations, the Heavenly Stems and the Earthly Branches. A compass has 360 degrees and eight major directions, each containing forty-five degrees of the compass. They are referred to as the eight cardinal directions: North, South, East, West, North East, North West, South East and South West. Each cardinal direction is segmented into three fifteen-degree sections. Three sections multiplied by eight cardinal directions produces twenty-four sections. Each section is called a "Mountain," and there are twenty-four Mountains on a standard Flying Stars Feng Shui compass. The following tables list each of the eight cardinal directions and their forty-five-degree areas, or palaces.

North West 292.5 – 337.5	North 337.5 – 22.5	North East 22.5 – 67.5
North West 1 292.5 – 307.5	North 1 337.5 – 352.5	North East 1 22.5 – 37.5
North West 2 307.5 – 322.5	North 2 352.5 – 7.5	North East 2 37.5 – 52.5
North West 3 322.5 – 337.5	North 3 7.5 – 22.5	North East 3 52.5 – 67.5
West 247.5 – 292.5	Center	East 67.5 – 112.5
West 1 247.5 – 262.5		East 1 67.5 – 82.5
West 2 262.5 – 277.5		East 2 82.5 – 97.5
West 3 277.5 – 292.5		East 3 97.5 – 112.5
South West 202.5 – 247.5	South 157.5 – 202.5	South East 112.5 – 157.5
South West 1 202.5 – 217.5	South 1 157.5 – 172.5	South East 1 12.5 – 127.5
South West 2 217.5 – 232.5	South 2 172.5 – 187.5	South East 2 127.5 – 142.5
South West 3 232.5 – 247.5	South 3 187.5 – 202.5	South East 3 142.5 – 157.5

Luo Pan Positions

Lo-Pan Position	Lo-Pan Position
North 1 337.5-352.5	South 1 157.5-172.5
North 2 352.5-7.5	South 2 172.5-187.5
North 3 7.5-22.5	South 3 187.5-202.5
North East 1 22.5-37.5	South West 1 202.5-217.5
North East 2 37.5-52.5	South West 2 217.5-232.5
North East 3 52.5-67.5	South West 3 232.5-247.5
East 1 67.5-82.5	West 1 247.5-262.5
East 2 82.5-97.5	West 2 262.5-277.5
East 3 97.5-112.5	West 3 277.5-292.5
South East 1 112.5-127.5	North West 1 292.5-307.5
South East 2 127.5-142.5	North West 2 307.5-322.5
South East 3 142.5-157.5	North West 3 322.5-337.5

Luo Pan, Chinese Feng Shui Compass for Twenty-four Mountains

Direction	Direction Gua	Mountain Polarity	Directional Gua Element	Stem, Branch or Trigram	Compass Degrees
North 1	Kan 1	Yang	Water	Ren—Yang Water	337.5–352.5
North 2	Kan 2	Yin	Water	Zi—Rat	352.5–7.5
North 3	Kan 3	Yin	Water	Gui—Yin Water	7.5–22.5
North East 1	Gen 1	Yin	Earth	Zhou—Ox	22.5–37.5
North East 2	Gen 2	Yang	Earth	Gen—Mountain	37.5–52.5
North East 3	Gen 3	Yang	Earth	Yin—Tiger	52.5–67.5
East 1	Zhen 1	Yang	Wood	Jia—Yang Wood	67.5–82.5
East 2	Zhen 2	Yin	Wood	Mao—Rabbit	82.5–97.5
East 3	Zhen 3	Yin	Wood	Yi—Yin Wood	97.5–112.5
South East 1	Xun 1	Yin	Wood	Zhen—Dragon	112.5–127.5
South East 2	Xun 2	Yang	Wood	Xun—Wood	127.5–142.5
South East 3	Xun 3	Yang	Wood	Si—Snake	142.5–157.5
South 1	Li 1	Yang	Fire	Bing—Yang Fire	157.5–172.5
South 2	Li 2	Yin	Fire	Wu—Horse	172.5–187.5
South 3	Li 3	Yin	Fire	Ding—Yin Fire	187.5–202.5
South West 1	Kun 1	Yin	Earth	Wei—Sheep	202.5–217.5
South West 2	Kun 2	Yang	Earth	Kun—Earth	217.5–232.5
South West 3	Kun 3	Yang	Earth	Shen—Monkey	232.5–247.5
West 1	Dui 1	Yang	Metal	Geng—Yang Metal	247.5–262.5
West 2	Dui 2	Yin	Metal	You—Cock	262.5–277.5
West 3	Dui 3	Yin	Metal	Xin—Yin Metal	277.5–292.5
North West 1	Qian 1	Yin	Metal	Xu—Dog	292.5–307.5
North West 2	Qian 2	Yang	Metal	Qian—Metal	307.5–322.5
North West 3	Qian 3	Yang	Metal	Hai—Pig	322.5–337.5

Building Orientation

Sitting-Mountain and Facing-Water positions are determined with a compass and are opposite each other. The terms Mountain/Sitting and Water/Facing are used interchangeably throughout this book—these two positions determine a building's orientation. In most cases, the front door will be the Facing-Water position and its opposite the Sitting-Mountain position. A Luo Pan compass reveals the relationship between each Mountain and Facing-Water position. When a Mountain or Facing-Water position is determined, its opposite position is automatically known. This relationship is referred to as Mountain/Water directions or Facing/Sitting directions.

The initial objective in Feng Shui is to determine a building's orientation, which means finding its structure or alignment; the following are guidelines for determining Facing and Sitting directions:

1. The front door direction is often the Facing direction. In some cases it will be another direction. Stand with your back to the front door. The direction straight ahead is the Facing direction and the direction to the back is the Sitting direction.

Often, a street or road in front of the structure is the Facing or Water direction. This is called the Yang direction of a building. The Facing direction is often positioned near the building entrance and the windows near the entry, front door or where the most sunlight is located. Combine this knowledge of building orientation and street location to accurately determine the Facing orientation.

2. Place a compass in your hands and keep it flat or parallel to the
    ground. Some compasses will automatically align the arrow in the
    middle to North-South; others have a movable dial which needs to
    be turned until the arrow in the middle is aligned to North-South.
    The front of the compass will have a mark, usually an arrow on the
    outside of the compass. The arrow will point at a degree on the
    dial. This degree is the Water or Facing direction and its exact
    opposite degree is the Mountain or Sitting direction. The dials of
    some compasses have one red end and one white—red is usually
    North, but you should confirm whether or not this is correct for
    your compass.

3. Metal can alter a compass's accuracy. It is important to remove
    metal or jewelry and stand away from major metal or electric
    structures, for example, telephone lines, metal stairways or auto-
    mobiles.

4. It is suggested that you take three or more readings in different
    locations along the same axis or facing the same direction—this
    should eliminate potential influences that may alter a compass
    reading. If the reading is consistent in numerous positions, the
    compass has not been influenced.

5. Remember, each of the twenty-four Mountains consists of fifteen-
    degree distances; if the compass reading falls within this range the
    reading is accurate. The dial does not have to show the exact degree
    reading each time; it only needs to fall within the fifteen- degree
    range.

6   **Finding a Flying Stars Feng Shui Chart**
    The pieces of information required to locate a Flying Stars Feng
    Shui chart are the twenty-year construction cycle Number, (1-9)

and the sitting position, for example, North 1, South 2, North East 3, West 2. The appendix contains Flying Stars Feng Shui charts for all of the twenty year periods, each chart is labelled with any special relevant chart information. Locate the construction period, then the Sitting Mountain to find your chart.

Locate the twenty year time frame your building was constructed or completed in the table below, the assocociated Cycle number (1-9) is the construction cycle. Locate the construction cycle in the Flying Stars Feng Shui charts in the Appendix, then the Sitting Mountain to find your building's chart.

Cycle	Years
1	1864-1883
2	1884-1903
3	1904-1923
4	1924-1943
5	1944-1963
6	1964-1983
7	1984-2003
8	2004-2023
9	2024-2043

Flying Stars

There are nine special influences in Flying Stars Feng Shui and they are referred to as stars. Each star is not really a physical star, but a representation of the energetic qualities or influences of nature. A number, trigram, color and other basic attributes represent each star, and some change with cycles of time. The following table lists each star.

Nine Stars

	Star	Basic Nature
1	White Star	Favorable
2	Black Star	Unfavorable
3	Green Star	Unfavorable
4	Dark Green Star	Unfavorable
5	Yellow Star	Unfavorable
6	White Star	Favorable
7	Red Star	Unfavorable
8	White Star	Favorable
9	Purple Star	Favorable

The basic quality of stars 1,6,8 and 9 are favorable. Stars 2, 3, 4, 5 and 7 are unfavorable. Star 5 is the most unfavorable, followed by star 2.

The basic nature of each star is the condition of the star when it is in a neutral condition, at any given time the meaning of each star is determined by the timeliness of the star. The concept of the time and condition of a star will be explained fully. Timeliness is of primary importance when determining the quality of stars and their meaning at a specific time.

Nine-Star Timeliness

Stars are a type of energy, or Qi, and reflect influences that affect one's life. This Qi moves through cycles of birth, growth and decline and exerts favorable and unfavorable influences. The cause of these different influences is "timeliness." When Qi, or a star, is timely, the favorable aspects manifest; when Qi, or a star, is untimely, unfavorable aspects may manifest. The Timely Water Star is called "Water Dragon Spirit" or "Shui Li Long Shen" and the Timely Mountain Star is called "Mountain Dragon Spirit" or "Shan Li Long Shen."

The Chinese calendar is the foundation for Asian arts. Feng Shui uses two major cycles. The first is a twenty-year cycle and the second is an annual cycle. Each twenty years a new cycle begins and is referred to as the Construction Year, or the Earth, Base or Time Star. Numbers or stars are assigned to each twenty-year cycle, and during those time frames its related star is the "Predominant" or "Timely Star." The table below lists each cycle with its corresponding number or star.

Stars and Their Related Twenty-year Cycle

Number	Twenty-year Cycle
1	1864–1883
2	1884–1903
3	1904–1923
4	1924–1943
5	1944–1963
6	1964–1983
7	1984–2003
8	2004–2023
9	2024–2043

Timeliness involves stages, and there are three main stages:

1. The first is Timely, or Wang. It is the current twenty-year cycle.

2. The second is Future Timely, or Sheng. It is the future twenty-year cycle.

3. The third is Distant Future Timely, or Sheng. It is the future forty- to sixty-year cycle.

For example, 1984–2003 is Cycle Seven. The Seven Star is most timely and most favorable during the 1984–2003 cycle. Star Eight is Future Timely, or the time frame which is next, and it is favorable as the energy is close and its influence is strong. Star Nine is in the distant future and is favorable because its energy will follow soon. Six Star, the Distant Past Star, reverts to its basic nature, but the energy is weak and does not exert a strong influence. All other stars revert to their untimely qualities except two stars, which are "safe" and "usable." This is explained later in the book. The following tables show the timeliness of each star for Cycle Seven, 1984–2003 and Cycle Eight, 2004-2023.

Timeliness During Cycle Seven (1984–2003)

Star	Timeliness
1	Untimely (Safe)
2	Untimely
3	Untimely
4	Untimely (Safe)
5	Distant Untimely
6	Close Distant Untimely Reverts to Basic Nature
7	Timely
8	Future Timely
9	Distant Future Timely

Timeliness During Cycle Eight (2004–2023)

Star	Timeliness
1	Sheng - Distant Future Timely
2	Untimely
3	Untimely (Safe and Usable)
4	Untimely
5	Untimely
6	Untimely (Safe and Usable)
7	Close Distant Untimely Reverts to Basic Nature
8	Wang - Timely
9	Sheng - Future Timely

** Safe and usable stars will be explained in the book. There is not a lot of Qi in these stars, so they can not generate prosperity in themselves, but will not cause problems. They do provide a safe environment for Water and Mountain placement, based on non-Flying Stars Feng Shui methods.**

Nine Stars in Timely and Untimely Cycles

Star	Five Element	Timely	Untimely	Disease
1	Water	Wealth, money, fame, spirituality, wisdom, philosophy	Divorce, death, isolation, miscarriage, impotency, sexual problems, mental instability	Kidneys, Ears, Blood
2	Earth	Fertility, leadership, high productivity	Sickness, potential miscarriage, digestive difficulties, loneliness	Stomach, Spleen, Abdomen, Digestion
3	Wood	Wealth, prosperity, growth, youth, leadership	Gossip, arguments, lawsuits, slander, robbers, disability	Feet, Lungs, Convulsions, Hysteria
4	Wood	Academic success, intelligence, creativity, artistic skills, fame, good fortune	Divorce, family pressure, affairs, infidelity, manipulation	Buttock, Thigh, Colds, Flu
5	Earth	Sudden wealth, prosperity, fame	Disease, pain, sickness, potential disaster, most negative energy, lack knowledge, laziness	Spleen, Stomach, digestion, all kinds of illness
6	Metal	Wealth, leadership, success, ambition, kindness, success in technology & science	Isolation, loneliness, sadness, blockages in all areas of life	Pulmonary disease, Headaches
7	Metal	Wealth, fertility, great verbal skills and languages, divination	Robbery, bleeding, arguing, fire, bickering, isolation, promiscuous, legal problems, STDs	Head, Lungs
8	Earth	Fame, wealth, spirituality, success for young people and family unity	Children may have injuries, loneliness, boredom, and reversal of fortune	Hands, Fingers, Back
9	Fire	Achievement, success, growth	Eye disease, fires, mental disturbance, miscarriage, and employment difficulties	Heart, Eyes

Early and Later Heaven Ba Gua

Usable Flying Stars

For each twenty-year cycle, the Time Star has two associated stars that are usable and safe, even if they are untimely by definition. The chart below lists each cycle with its Timely and Usable Stars, which is followed by detailed explanations of this theory.

Safe and Usable Stars

Number	Twenty-Year Cycle	Timely Star	Usable Stars
1	1864–1883	1	Stars 2, 7
2	1884–1903	2	Stars 1, 4
3	1904–1923	3	Stars 8, 9
4	1924–1943	4	Stars 2, 7
5	1944–1963	5	Stars 2, 8
6	1964–1983	6	Stars 8, 9
7	1984–2003	7	Stars 1, 4
8	2004–2023	8	Stars 3, 6
9	2024–2043	9	Stars 3, 6

Early Heaven Ba Gua

South East *Dui* *7*	*South* *Qian* *6*	*South West* *Xun* *4*
East *Li* *9*	*Center* *Earth*	*West* *Kan* *1*
North East *Zhen* *3*	*North* *Kun* *2*	*North West* *Gen* *8*

Later Heaven Ba Gua

South East *4*	*South* *9*	*South West* *2*
East *3*	 *5*	*West* *7*
North East *8*	*North* *1*	*North West* *6*

1. During 1984–2003, or Cycle Seven, Timely Star Seven is located in the West in the Later Heaven Ba Gua. Locate the trigram number in the West in the Early Heaven Ba Gua (it is Kan, or 1).

2. For Cycle Seven, locate Star Seven in the Early Heaven Ba Gua. It is in the South East. Locate the trigram in the South East in the Later Heaven Ba Gua. (It is 4, or Xun.)

3. Kan-1 and Xun-4 are the two usable stars for Cycle Seven; they are the associated stars for Cycle Seven in the Early and Later Heaven Ba Guas.

The following table combines the Early Heaven and Later Heaven Ba Guas. It combines usable stars for each palace and their associated time frames.

Early and Later Heaven Ba Guas Combined

South East	South	South West
Dui 7	Qian 6	Xun 4
Xun 4	Li 9	Kun 2
East	Center	West
Li 9	Earth	Kan 1
Zhen 3		Dui 7
North East	North	North West
Zhen 3	Kun 2	Gen 8
Gen 8	Kan 1	Qian 6

- The Early Heaven arrangement is located in the top row and the Later Heaven trigrams are located in the lower row.

This Flying Star Feng Shui method is applicable in all nine cycles.

Five-Element Remedies

Five-Element relationships constitute a major method for harmonizing Flying Stars Feng Shui situations. Each palace contains a Mountain-Sitting Star, a Water-Facing Star and a Time Star, and each Star represents one of the Five Elements. Interactions between stars will be either supporting, reducing, producing or controlling. The table below lists recommended Five-Element remedies.

Element	Color	Shapes and Remedies
Water	Black, Blue	curvy, wavy, cascading shapes aquarium, fountains, swimming pools
Wood	Green	beam or rod shapes plants, flowers
Fire	Red, Purple, Pink, Orange	triangle, pyramid shapes red candles, lamp with red shades, red objects, red light
Earth	Yellow, Beige, Brown, Tan	square, flat shapes soil, rocks, crystals, ceramics, porcelain
Metal	White, Gold, Silver	round, circles, sphere shapes grandfather clock, metal chimes, coins, metal objects

Nine Stars

Facing, Sitting and twenty-year construction cycle stars exist in each of the Nine Places and have individual and group meetings. Analyzing these stars is an integral aspect of Flying Stars Feng Shui. The following principles are a guide for working with the stars:

- Stars represent potential. There is a possibility they will manifest, but they generally require activators to cause them to come alive and actually manifest in one's life.

- Sometimes activators are in the environment and stars do not manifest, and other times they do. A Feng Shui practitioner needs to evaluate all aspects of Feng Shui to determine what is occurring and determine if the cause originates from Feng Shui. External forms, interior design, Five-Element items and timeliness are vital factors in Feng Shui.

  View the stars as internal organs and the forms and Five-Element remedies as blood and energy, which brings life to organs. Stars alone are like organs in a dead body—there is no life force in them. External and Internal forms are activators that provide life force which can activate stars or diminish them.

- External Forms are most potent and influence living environments—they have a Qi influence of their own which can be favorable or unfavorable and have a unique influence in conjunction with Flying Stars.

- Annual and monthly stars can activate stars in the palaces they enter.

- Buildings can be prioritized according to their potential to promote prosperity; from a Flying Stars Feng Shui perspective, the Facing and Sitting palaces are most important. If the stars are favorable in these palaces, the entire building will have a strong favorable influence, since the Facing Palace reflects wealth for the entire building and the Sitting Palace reflects health and relationships for the entire building.

  If these palaces are unfavorable, it is important to eliminate or reduce unfavorable forms and stars and activate favorable stars in other palaces, especially the timely stars. In addition to activating favorable stars, it is very important to use "Special Prosperity" methods to transcend the influences of the Facing and Sitting palaces; methods included in this book are Primary and Secondary Fortune palaces, He Tu Castle Gate, Castle Gate, Water and Mountain Fan Gua and Five Ghosts Carry Money.

The following tables list the meanings of the Nine Stars during cycles Seven and Eight. Refer to them for possible influences in living environments:

Meanings of Stars for Cycle 7
1984–2003

Timely and Favorable Stars: Seven, Eight, Nine
Neutral Stars: One, Four, Six
Untimely and Unfavorable: Two, Three, Five

Star	Star Element	Meaning	Disease
1	Water	Wealth, money, fame, spirituality, wisdom, philosophy	Kidneys, Ears, Blood
2	Earth	Sickness, potential miscarriage, digestive difficulties, loneliness	Stomach, Spleen, Abdomen, Digestion
3	Wood	Gossip, arguments, lawsuits, slander, robbers, disability	Feet, Lungs, Convulsions, Hysteria
4	Wood	Academic success, intelligence, creativity, artistic skills, fame, good fortune	Buttock, Thigh, Colds, Flu
5	Earth	Disease, pain, sickness, potential disaster, most negative energy, lack of knowledge, laziness	Spleen, Stomach, digestion, all kinds of illness.
6	Metal	Wealth, leadership, success, ambition, success in technology & science	Pulmonary disease, Headaches
7	Metal	Wealth, fertility, great verbal skills and languages, divination	Head, Lungs
8	Earth	Fame, wealth, spirituality, success for young people and family unity	Hands, Fingers, Back, Spine
9	Fire	Achievement, success, growth	Heart, Eyes

Meanings of Stars for Period Eight
2004–2023

Timely and Favorable Stars: Eight, Nine, One
Neutral Stars: Three, Six
Untimely: Two, Four, Five, Seven

Star	Star Element	Meaning	Disease
1	Water	Wealth, money, fame, spirituality, wisdom, philosophy	Kidneys, Ears, Blood
2	Earth	Sickness, potential miscarriage, digestive difficulties, loneliness	Stomach, Spleen, Abdomen, Digestion
3	Wood	Wealth, prosperity, growth, youth, leadership	Feet, Lungs, Convulsions, Hysteria
4	Wood	Divorce, family pressure, affairs, infidelity, manipulation	Buttock, Thigh, Colds, Flu
5	Earth	Disease, pain, sickness, potential disaster, most negative energy, lack knowledge, laziness	Spleen, Stomach, digestion, all kinds of illness
6	Metal	Wealth, leadership, success, ambition, success in technology & science	Pulmonary disease, Headaches
7	Metal	Robbery, bleeding, arguing, fire, bickering, isolation, promiscuous, legal problems, STDs	Head, Lungs
8	Earth	Fame, wealth, spirituality, success for young people and family unity	Hands, Fingers, Back
9	Fire	Achievement, success, growth	Heart, Eyes

- Activate the timely Eight, Nine and One stars.
- In the areas containing untimely stars Two, Four, Five and Seven, avoid important activities, keep quiet, do not stimulate

with forms or elements and apply Five-Element remedies to reduce stars, especially if the sitting star is being controlled. Health is most important.

Nine Star Combinations

The following star combinations may produce qualities that are different than their individual meanings. Sometimes two interacting stars create a synergy that cannot be explained by our standard evaluations of the stars; the following must be considered:

1. Stars are potential Qi, which can be activated by forms and Five-Element remedies. When they are activated, we must factor in timeliness to obtain their meanings.

2. Stars can be categorized as guest or host:

    •   When considering Wealth, the Facing or Water Star is the host and the Mountain or Sitting Star is the guest. Time, Annual and Monthly Stars are also guest stars.

    •   When considering Health, Relationships or Fertility, the Sitting or Mountain Star is the host and the Water or Facing Star is the guest. The Time, Annual and Monthly Stars are also guest stars.

3. Consider the original Five-Element energy in each palace and how it affects the host and guests Stars. Does it support, diminish or control stars? This is a minor influence which is used to measure the potency of stars in a palace. It assists in determining how strong they vibrate, and can be favorable or unfavorable.

4. Forms surrounding a structure have a profound effect on stars—they can trigger them in unfavorable or favorable ways.

5. Forms inside the structure (interior design) have a profound effect on stars—they can trigger them in unfavorable or favorable ways.

6. For more information, refer to the trigrams and their correspondences.

7. Stars can be evaluated in a rigid or broad way. The rigid way is when a Sitting Star relates only to people and Water Star only to wealth. A broader way is when there is overlap between them.

8. Forms, both exterior and interior, can activate Facing-Sitting or Water-Mountain Stars. Annual, Monthly, Sitting, Facing and Time Stars in each palace can combine, creating "Star Combinations." They are an integral part of Flying Stars Feng Shui.

The following are the eighty-one star combinations. Please refer to these combinations as well as their individual meanings to obtain a comprehensive understanding of Flying Stars Feng Shui.

Star Combination	Meanings
1,1	Romance, affairs, alcoholism, legal problems, scholastic achievement
1,2	Spousal/relationship difficulties, female domination, gynecological problems, potential automobile accidents
1,3	Gossip, arguments, lawsuits, loss of money, tempers are activated, success when traveling
1,4	Romance for women, intelligence, use a small amount of non-moving water as a remedy
1,5	Womb and genital problems, food and fluid poisoning
1,6	Good for middle son and their good fortune, scholastic achievement, intelligent children
1,7	Romance
1,8	Trouble with business partners
1,9	Venereal disease, changes jobs/careers, heart disease

Star Combination	Meanings
2,1	Gynecological disorders, abortion, diminished sex drive, infertility, spousal relationship difficulties-the women may be too controlling
2,2	Miscarriage
2,3	Bullfighting Combination, gossip, arguments, lawsuits, digestive and abdominal problems, especially older females, serious situations, family troubles, avoid using this area of a building or room
2,4	Unfavorable sexual encounters for young females, mother/daughter in-law problems, others cause emotional stress
2,5	Most Serious situation, health (particularly abdominal), cancer, miscarriages, financial disaster, illness, accidents, take no action, avoid this area, pay close attention to annual and monthly stars which may activate this Star combination.
2,6	Pain, Sickness (especially abdominal), blockages
2,7	If 9 Star enters a possible Fire
2,8	Good for real estate, possible monk/ nun or loner, good financial prospects
2,9	Romance/ peach blossom for women, potential eye problems

Star Combination	Meanings
3,1	Theft, loss of money, possible violence
3,2	Possible auto accident, females get sick easy, mother-son difficulties, avoid this area of a building or room
3,3	Possible theft, cold disposition
3,4	Mental-Emotional Difficulties, males attract females, difficulties for elderly females, theft
3,5	Difficulties with money, unfavorable for young males, auto accidents, infectious diseases, loss when gambling
3,6	Difficulties for young adults, leg problems, car accidents, headaches, accidents with sharp objects
3,7	Robbery, betrayal
3,8	Difficulties with young children, possible miscarriage, homosexuality
3,9	Birth of intelligent baby, robbery, possible fire accident

Star Combination	Meanings
4,1	Romance for females, possible affairs, academic and literary success
4,2	Unfavorable sexual affairs for women, mother-daughter in-law problems, unfavorable for elderly females, others cause stress
4,3	Good for arts, unfavorable affairs, males attract females
4,4	Attract the opposite sex, travel
4,5	Skin disease, pain, infectious disease, gambling, breast cancer
4,6	Possible miscarriage, colds, flu, relationship breakups, loss of wife
4,7	Possible miscarriage, divorce, injury with sharp objects, pregnant women, favorable love affairs, turmoil between women
4,8	Back problems, good for real estate
4,9	Male child is a genius, caution about fire accidents, female homosexuality

Star Combination	Meanings
5,1	Bladder problems, reproductive difficulties, ear diseases, pain, blockage, food poisoning
5,2	Most serious condition, widow, widower, pain, illness, stay away from this space, keep it inactive, pay close attention to annual and monthly stars which may activate this area
5,3	Illness (especially of the eldest son), unfavorable for youths, bankruptcy, loss of money, deception
5,4	Skin disease, flu, viruses, loss of money due to gambling
5,5	Serious situation, illness, blockages, accidents
5,6	Head problems, lung diseases, impotence
5,7	Mouth related problems, food poisoning, sexual diseases
5,8	Paralysis, emotional disorders
5,9	Poison, eye difficulties, ulcer, caution when gambling or investing, caution about fire accidents

Star Combination	Meanings
6,1	Peach blossom, favorable for writing and the middle son, cunning, good for career growth
6,2	Blockages especially in career and money, abdominal diseases, gynecological problems
6,3	Unfavorable for young people, lower limb problems, auto accidents, headache
6,4	Relationship difficulties, loneliness, broken hearts
6,5	Natural disasters, lung disease, serous disease, men stress over career
6,6	Difficulties with family members
6,7	"Double Metal Clash", Males fight with each other, robbery
6,8	Possible loneliness, emotional disorders
6,9	"Fire Burns Heaven Gate", bickering with the elderly, toothache, high blood pressure, trouble with sons, do not have kitchen stove here, lung disease, head of family has many problems

Star Combination	Meanings
7,1	Romance, possible affairs, good for travel
7,2	Infertility, females argue
7,3	Robbery, loss of money
7,4	Romance, good for travel
7,5	Arguing, deception, STD's, emotional disorders, unfavorable sexual behavior
7,6	Skin disease, jealousy, arguing
7,7	Robbery, possible unfavorable affairs for men
7,8	Romance, success in competition, sudden money
7,9	Possible fire and heart disease, flirting, irritable disposition

Star Combination	Meanings
8,1	Arguments among partners
8,2	Potential miscarriage, nun/monk types, loss of money
8,3	Difficult for young kids (under 12)
8,4	Difficult for young kids, difficulty having kids and getting married, martial stress
8,5	Paralysis, serious illness
8,6	Easily emotional upset
8,7	Good for young females and males in relationships during cycle 7
8,8	Great for real estate
8,9	Joyful activities including marriage

Star Combination	Meanings
9,1	Venereal disease, peach blossom, change jobs, heart and eye problems, miscarriage, academic success
9,2	Unfavorable for children, gynecological problems, fertility difficulties
9,3	Possible fire accidents and robberies
9,4	Caution for fire accidents, unfavorable sexual relations
9,5	Negative for gambling and investments, possible eye problems, rigid personality
9,6	"Fire Burns Heaven Gate", do not have kitchen stove here, arguments with the elderly, avoid fire mountain in the forms near this palace, lung disease, head of family has lots of stress Remedy: Add Earth
9,7	Fertility, possible fires
9,8	Good for joyful activities and marriage
9,9	Good for activities that have the nature of change: fashion, toys, etc.

Flying Stars and Forms

The key elements of Flying Stars Feng Shui are time, space, interior design and forms. Forms include environmental factors and interior design. In Flying Stars Feng Shui, a key factor is the location of mountains and water, which can be real or virtual.

The combination of form and Flying Stars Feng Shui Stars create favorable and unfavorable influences. The following external forms are guidelines for favorable Feng Shui:

- The Timely Facing Star is located in the Facing position in the Facing Palace. Water is located in front of the Facing Palace to activate this auspicious star.

- The Timely Sitting Star is located in the sitting position in the Sitting Palace. Mountain is located behind the Mountain Palace to activate this auspicious star.

- Timely Water Stars want to see water in all cycles. Water activates the timely stars. If one is trained in the Five Elements and is concerned the element will reduce the Five-Element of the timely star, use virtual water.

- Timely Mountain Stars want to see mountain in all cycles. Mountain activates the Mountain Star. If one is trained in the Five Elements and is concerned the element will reduce the Five-Element of the timely star, use virtual water.

- It is important to realize stars are Qi and may or may not manifest their qualities. Sometimes one will make remedies to activate the stars and they will not manifest. This is a normal phenomenon; if it happens, one should try alternate methods or remedies, or change the quantity or quality, or change the location of the placement within the forty-five-degree palace. The placement within in a palace should be within a fifteen-degree Mountain location. Sometimes it is a matter of placing a remedy a few degrees to the right or left, that is often the difference between a small and substantial result.

The table below lists Water and Mountain remedies in two ways. The first lists real examples and the second virtual. Real water and mountains are most powerful, while virtual water and mountains are not as effective.

Water-Mountain Forms

Element	Real	Virtual
Water	River, Lake, Fountains, Aquariums (Moving Water is best.)	Road, Flatland, Hallways, Lower Ground, *Activity*
Mountain	Mountains, Hills, High Ground	Buildings, Walls, *Inactivity*

Evaluate the influence of mountain or water on the stars in the palace and select locations or create the proper forms only if they are in harmony with the stars. Proper forms are critical in Flying Stars Feng Shui and activate both timely and untimely stars; if an Untimely Mountain Star is located in the Mountain Palace and there is a mountain behind the palace, it will activate or trigger this untimely star. The harmony between forms and Flying Stars Feng Shui is called "He Ju," which means, "forms activating the auspicious Qi of the Stars." Some use the term, "Dragon Method" to refer to the style and influence of mountains. When they say, "Mountain Dragon is satisfied," they mean the mountain form properly activates stars.

Water needs to be managed carefully because it represents activity and stimulates Qi. Water can create favorable and unfavorable activities. For example, water can activate an Untimely Water Star. Ideally, the Timely Facing Star should be supported by water forms, including actual water, lower ground and open areas like streets, flatlands, valleys and hallways. Ideally, mountain forms, including mountains, hills and highlands, should support the Timely Mountain Star.

Flying Stars Feng Shui and Interior Forms

Interior design in Flying Stars Feng Shui follows the basic principles of water- and mountain-form remedies. Interior design water forms include corridors, hallways, doors and passageways and should be located with Timely Facing Stars as they activate them. Interior design mountain forms include walls, rooms, partitions, stairs (walls) and large static objects and should be located with Timely Mountain Stars to activate them.

- Timely Facing Stars should have water interior design forms to activate them.

- Timely Mountain Stars should have mountain interior design forms to activate them.

- Avoid activating Untimely Water and Mountain Stars with interior forms.

Flying Stars Charts

There are many Feng Shui methods for harmonizing living environments. Some are integrated and part of a specific system, while others stand alone. We can view a building and its surrounding environment as an energy field, one which may be influenced by different methods to promote favorable results. The following describes a prevalent and potent method within Flying Stars Feng Shui.

Individual stars and their combinations are one aspect of Flying Stars Feng Shui. Another integral aspect of Feng Shui is the configuration, pattern or arrangement of the Flying Stars in a chart—they reveal a deep and influential aspect of Feng Shui. The following four types, or styles, of Flying Stars Feng Shui charts are primary charts and will be found in all Flying Stars Charts.

1. Prosperous Stars in the Sitting and Facing Palaces—Wang Shan Wang Shui

2. Prosperous Stars in Reversed Positions— Shang Shan Xia Shui

3. Double Stars meet in the Facing Palace—Xing Dao Xiang

4. Double Stars meet in the Sitting Palace- Xing Dao Zuo

Feng Shui practitioners agree the special qualities for these structures exist during the twenty years of the construction period, the first twenty years of its life. Others believe when the twenty-year construction cycle is over the special qualities listed no longer exist and other methods to optimize the building are needed. Some believe the chart qualities last longer—it is my experience that the Flying Star's aspect of these charts reaches their height in the twenty years of the original construction cycle. The reason the chart is most powerful at this time is that the timely stars are located in some type of distribution in the Facing and Sitting Palaces, which influence the wealth, health and relationships for the entire building. When the twenty-year construction period is over, the timeliness of the stars in the Facing And Sitting Palaces may become untimely, therefore unfavorably influencing the building.

- Each building must be re-evaluated when a new twenty-year cycle begins to identify timely and untimely stars and create favorable forms and remedies.

- In the appendix, Flying Stars Feng Shui charts for all the twenty-year cycles are listed along with their type of chart. This includes special formations for Cycle Eight, 2004–2023.

The following guideline for Flying Stars water and mountain placement should be applied to the following Flying Stars Feng Shui charts:

1. Prosperous Stars in the Sitting and Facing Palaces—Wang Shan Wang Shui

2. Prosperous Stars in Reversed Positions— Shang Shan Xia Shui

3. Double Stars meet in the Facing Palace—Xing Dao Xiang

4. Double Stars meet in the Sitting Palace- Xing Dao Zuo

5. Sum to Ten

6.   Fu Mu San Gua—Parent String

7.   Lin Chu San Pan Kua—Pearl String

The method for identifying each of these four types of charts is based on the location of the twenty-year construction cycle stars. Each chart will have three stars for each of the Nine Stars (for example, three ones, three twos, three threes or three fours for a normal chart). This is because we float the Construction, Sitting and Facing Stars through each palace, generating a complete cycle of Nine Stars. *The three Time or Construction-Year Stars will always be located in some variation in the Center, Facing and Sitting Palaces.* The order, or flow, of those stars determines a specific type of Flying Stars Feng Shui chart. The distribution of the Time Stars is a code that reveals some of the most powerful influences of the Flying Stars.

The ideal form correction should be placed outside the building in the surrounding area. One can view forms as a potent source of Qi, far stronger than small Five-Element remedies. It is necessary to evaluate the external forms to determine if they have an unfavorable or favorable influence. This is an important diagnostic method.

The following are examples for each of the four major types of charts, or Flying Stars formations. Some charts need form corrections, which consist of the proper placement of water and mountain.

Water corrections include oceans, lakes, streams, fountains, ponds, swimming pools, flatlands, streets and hallways.

Mountain corrections include mountains, hills, buildings, earth-based sculptures, rocks and soil.

1. Prosperous Stars in the Sitting and Facing Palaces—Wang Shan Wang Shui

Facing Direction

	North *Facing Palace* *Sitting Facing* $\underline{7}$	
West	$\underline{7}$	*East*
	Sitting Facing $\underline{7}$ *Sitting Palace* South	

Sitting Direction

In this situation, the Sitting and Facing Stars are in their proper positions. The Twenty-year Construction Cycle Star is Seven—this is referred to as the *Time Star*. When a Time Star is in the Facing position in the Facing Palace, another Time Star will be located in the Sitting position in the Sitting Palace. This reflects the proper distribution and influence of the timely stars. The underlying influence is good for health and wealth.

A Wang Shan Wang Shui structure increases the magnitude of favorable stars and decreases the magnitude of unfavorable stars. The Timely

Facing Star vibrates strongly in the Facing Palace, influencing wealth throughout the entire building. The same is true for the Timely Sitting Star.

The proper forms for this structure are water located in front of the Facing Palace to activate the Facing Star and mountain or earth behind the Sitting palace to activate the Sitting Star. Ideally, both should be located outside the physical building. This remedy is for the twenty-year construction cycle only. After this cycle, the building needs to be revaluated.

2.   Prosperous Stars in Reversed Positions— Shang Shan Xia Shui

Facing Direction

	North Facing Palace	
	Sitting Facing <u>7</u>	
West		East
	<u>7</u>	
	Sitting Facing <u>7</u> Sitting Palace South	

Sitting Direction

In this situation, the Facing and Sitting Stars are in reversed order. The Twenty-Year Construction Cycle Star is Seven and is referred to as the Time Star. When a Time Star is in the Sitting position in the Facing Palace, another Time Star will be located in the Facing position in the Sitting palace. This reflects a reversed distribution and influence of the Time Star.

The method to promote prosperity for this chart is to have a mountain or earth element in front of the Facing part of the structure (to activate the Mountain Star) and Water behind the Sitting-Mountain position of the structure (to activate the Water Star). If proper forms already exist in the environment, no additional remedies are necessary. This remedy is for the twenty-year construction cycle only. After this cycle, the building needs to be revaluated.

3. Double Stars meet in the Facing Palace—Xing Dao Xiang

Facing Direction

	North Facing Palace Sitting Facing $\underline{7}$ $\underline{7}$	
West	7	East
	Sitting Facing Sitting Palace South	

Sitting Direction

In this chart formation, timely stars are in the Sitting and Facing positions in the facing palace and are not optimally located. All Time Stars are in the Facing or Water Palace and are favorable for wealth.

The proper placement for a "Double Stars Meet in the Facing Palace" is to have mountain or earth in front of the Facing direction to activate the Mountain Star, and water in the front, as well, to activate the Water Star. These two form placements activate both stars in the Facing palace. This remedy is used for the twenty-year construction cycle only. After this cycle, the building needs to be revaluated.

4. Double Stars meet in the Sitting—Xing Dao Zuo

Facing Direction

	North *Facing Palace* Sitting Facing	
West	 7 	East
	Sitting Facing <u>7</u> <u>7</u> *Sitting Palace* South	

Sitting Direction

In this situation, the two timely stars, or Twenty-Year Construction Cycle Stars, are placed in the Sitting, or Mountain, Palace. The proper forms for a "Double Stars Meet in the Sitting Palace" is to place water behind the Sitting Palace of the structure to activate the Water Star and to place earth in this area as well to activate the Mountain Star. This remedy is used for the twenty-year construction cycle only. After this cycle, the building needs to be revaluated.

Locked Flying Star Chart

A locked, or Prison Flying Stars Chart, is when the timely or current-cycle star is in the Center Palace in the Sitting-Mountain or Facing-Water position. Locked buildings influence people and wealth. When they are not remedied, very unfavorable luck will affect the occupants and override favorable aspects of Feng Shui. The following explains this structure:

Locked Chart

	North *Facing Palace* *Sitting* *Facing*	
West	*Sitting* *Facing* <u>7</u> 6	*East*
	Sitting *Facing* *Sitting Palace* South	

In this case, the current period, or timely star, is located in the Center Palace in the Sitting position. Therefore this structure is locked in the Sitting-Mountain Position and the influence is unfavorable for health and people during cycle 7, 1984–2003, unless it is harmonized. *View a locked building as the timely star being trapped or locked in the center palace where it cannot be distributed to the eight geographical palaces. Its favorable influence cannot be expressed throughout the building.*

For the years 2004–2023, Eight is the timely star, and during Cycle Eight, Seven is distant untimely. If a Seven Star were in the Mountain or Facing position in the Center Palace, it would not be locked; only an Eight can be locked during 2004–2023. In other words, *only the timely or wang star can be locked.* Only the Eight Star can be locked during Period Eight, years 2004–2023.

If the Seven Star is located in the Facing position in the Center Palace, the Facing, water or wealth, aspect of life will be locked for Cycle 7, 1984–2003.

A locked structure will be unfavorable for either Health/Fertility/People, Relationships or Wealth unless the proper remedy is implemented.

See the Flying Stars charts in the back of the book. All charts locked in Period Eight are listed.

Locked Corrections

A structure is locked or in prison when the timely star is located in the Sitting or Facing position in the Center Palace. For example, during the years 2004-2023 Eight is the timely or wang star, if any building, regardless of when it was constructed, has a Eight star in the facing or sitting position in the center palace, it is a Locked chart. The goal is to release this timely star so it can favorably influence the building. One could say this pattern is part of the energetic DNA or blueprint of a structure—even if each of the key palaces contains favorable stars, they will not manifest unless the lock is released.

A locked building can unfavorably influence people or wealth, the entire building is influenced by Locked charts.

The following includes three remedies for locked structures:

First Remedy

1.   Identify whether the Facing or Sitting position is in prison. If the Facing position is in prison, locate Star Five in the Facing position in one of the Eight palaces. Every chart will have one palace containing a Five Star in the Sitting-Mountain and Facing-Water Positions. The only way they will be in the same palace is if the structure is a Double Facing or Double Sitting chart. If the physical area from the Center Palace to the palace containing Facing Star Five is open, with no obstructions, Star Seven, or the locked star, can fly and be released. In this situation, no corrections are necessary. Physical obstructions include walls, partitions or doors that separate the area from the Center Palace to the Five Star. This obstacle traps the imprisoned Seven Star.

Perform the same evaluation if the Mountain Star is in prison.

Some Feng Shui Masters place water in the Palace containing the Five Star; others believe the water may activate the Unfavorable Five Star.

Second Remedy

If a building is located close to and in view of a body of water (an ocean, lake, etc.), the star is released from prison; residents need to be able to see water from the building.

Third Remedy

Change Heaven's Heart

When evaluating a Flying Stars Feng Shui chart, the center has profound influences. The classics refer to the center as "Heaven's Heart." It influences the entire chart/building. The chart begins with the star relating to the Twenty-Year Construction Cycle, which is called the Time, Construction, Earth or Base Star.

Heaven's Heart has four major purposes:

1. The center is used to float the Twenty-Year Construction Number, which is the first step in constructing a Flying Stars Feng Shui chart.

2. The center is used to determine the type of Flying Stars structure.

3. The center contains information to determine whether a structure is in prison, or locked.

4. The center stars indicate any underlying influences on the total structure.

Heaven's Heart

One Flying Stars Feng Shui strategy to change the Qi of a building is to change Heaven's Heart. The following are a few methods to change Heaven's Heart:

1. If a structure's roof and ceiling is removed and then rebuilt, the time the new ceiling-roof is enclosed becomes the new Twenty-Year Construction Cycle. For example, a house built in 1925 is in Cycle Four; if the entire roof and ceiling is removed and replaced in 2009, it becomes a Construction Cycle Eight structure. Removing the ceiling means that if it were to rain, water would come inside the house and get the floor and furniture wet, or that sunlight would shine inside the house. The roof should be opened at least twenty-four hours (some believe it should be removed for seven days). This does not entail merely removing shingles or the top of the roof—the time the ceiling-roof encloses the structure is the time used for the Construction Cycle. Ideally, the front door is removed for the same duration as the roof.

    Changing the Twenty-Year Construction Cycle by removing the roof has two major applications. First, when remodeling takes place and a roof is replaced, a new chart must be calculated, evaluated and remedied. Second, when a building is in a good cycle and is entering a negative cycle, or is currently in a negative cycle, opening up a house creates a new twenty-year cycle and a new chart. By calculating the new chart before remodeling, it can be determined whether the new chart is favorable. If it is favorable, it is a strategic decision to remodel and create an auspicious environment.

If the structure is completed close to the beginning or end of a twenty-year cycle, the exact date must be determined. If the date cannot be determined and it is close to the transition time, calculate two charts, present the client with information about each chart and determine which is correct. This method is very effective.

2. Performing renovations includes removing part of the roof, removing and placing a new front door (the one actually used) and/or adding extensions—this can include a skylight greater than one-third the size of the original building.

3. One can change the location of the front door or the door actually used to a favorable position or mountain as determined by Flying Stars or special prosperity methods. This is changing the "Mouth of Qi", the first Qi to enter the building.

4. Modern practitioners have had success in modern living environments by changing windows and doors, remodeling rooms and painting the building if the more traditional and ideal methods are not possible.

The following are examples of locked structures:

1. Cycle Six, Sitting North West 2 during years 1984–2003—Star Seven is locked.

2. Cycle Seven, Sitting South East 1 during 2004–2023—Star Eight is locked.

3. Cycle Six, Sitting East 1 during 2004–2023-Star Eight is locked.

Special Case

If the Five Star is locked, select and perform one of the following remedies:

1. Change Heaven's Heart.

2. Activate Palaces containing the Future and Distant Future Timely Stars in the building.

3. If a large body of water is in sight, the lock is released.

Evaluating Palaces

The most important palaces and areas in a building are:

1. Facing Palace

   The Facing Palace reflects wealth and influences wealth throughout the entire building. The quality of the Water Star has a strong influence on the entire building.

2. Sitting Palace

   The Sitting Palace reflects health and relationships throughout the entire building. The quality of the Sitting Star has a strong influence on the entire building.

   If the Facing and Sitting Palaces are favorable then the building has a great chance to promote prosperity from a Flying Stars perspective. It is like having a good genetic condition.

3. Center Palace

   The Center Palace reveals special qualities about a building, for example, the style of the building and whether or not it is locked. The center palace is also called "Heaven's Heart."

4. Entrance

   The entrance is also called "Mouth of Qi." It is the entry of energy, or Qi, into the building. This Qi has a profound influence on the building.

If the Facing and Sitting Palaces and entrance are favorable, with good forms, the building is favorable.

5. Bedrooms

Bedrooms are where one spends many hours; the Qi in this area has a strong influence on health, relationships, career and wealth.

If the Facing and Sitting Palaces, entrance and master bedroom are favorable, the building has a strong potential for prosperity.

6. Where You Spend Time

View each area in a building as containing a Qi field. This Qi field influences each person, continually exerting the influence of Flying Stars, external forms and interior design.

When evaluating a building we can create levels of favorable and unfavorable influences. The following are general guidelines:

- A building is most favorable when:

    1. External forms create Sheng Qi, regardless of Flying Stars Feng Shui.

    2. External forms support Flying Stars charts.

3. Interior design supports Flying Stars and general Feng Shui principles.

4. Proper remedies are in the key palaces.

5. The Facing and Sitting Palaces, entrance and master bedroom are favorable.

Here is a general strategy for Feng Shui:

1. Select favorable external forms.

2. Select a Wang Shan Wang Shui chart and forms that activate the timely stars in the Facing and Sitting stars. This applies for the first twenty years of a building's life.

3. Select timely special charts, for example, Parent String, Pearl String and Sum to Ten. Be sure forms support these Flying Star formations.

4. Look for key areas of the building that have timely stars: entrance, master bedrooms, offices, places where one spends time—this is where we want favorable star and Qi.

5. If there is an unfavorable mountain form, try creating a wood element in the environment, as wood controls earth/mountain. This can include trees, shrubbery or beam/rod-shaped struc-tures. Additionally, metal can be added outside, as metal reduces earth/mountain.

6. If there is an unfavorable water form, try placing a wood element outside, as wood reduces water. Earth can be added to counter unfavorable water, as earth controls water.

7. In all cases, the real or elemental forms added should be in harmony with the Flying Stars.

8. If untimely stars are in the major areas of a building, harmonize the stars by creating favorable forms and applying Five-Element remedies, then use special prosperity methods that are not Flying Stars-based to promote prosperity. Select palaces where Flying Stars are favorable or neutral when applying the special prosperity methods; these methods influence the entire building, not just the palace where they are placed. There are seven methods in this book.

9. Use transcendental items to enhance one's environment. For example, if the Three Star is untimely and in the bedroom, place a picture that reflects beautiful communication skills to assist in your efforts to promote this quality.

10. For Cycle Eight, the standard forms to activate Wang Shan Wang Shui, Shang Shan Xia Shui, Xing Dao Xiang and Xing Da Zuo should be applied to buildings built only during the cycle 2004–2023; all buildings constructed in other cycles should have forms to activate timely stars and other relevant and timely principles.

Prosperity Methods

The roots of Feng Shui are in the *I Ching*, the oldest of Chinese books and the foundation of Chinese metaphysics and culture. Many applications of the *I Ching* have been kept a secret for centuries; only the most trusted students of a Masters' inner-circle have been exposed to the "Water Dragon" Feng Shui methods for promoting prosperity. Traditionally a student would spend many years before obtaining these ancient formulas, which are written in deep metaphor, preventing their understanding and implementation. The following methods include some of the most famous and potent Feng Shui methods for promoting prosperity. The methods are presented in a user-friendly method for placements in apartments, homes and offices. These methods offer opportunities, if they are in harmony with general Feng Shui principles apply them to your living spaces. These methods are not Flying Stars Feng Shui based, they tap into a different Qi and can transcend the influences of Flying Stars. It is important to realize these methods influence the entire building, not just the area of placement. Welcome to an ancient and powerful aspect of Feng Shui.

Primary Fortunate Palaces

Indirect Spirit (Ling Shen) Palaces

During each twenty-year cycle, certain directions (Wang directions) are prevalent. These special and potentially auspicious directions are based on the Later Heaven arrangement of the Ba Gua. Below is a later Heaven Ba Gua chart for years 1984–2003, which is Cycle Seven. Star Seven resides in the West Palace. Its opposite, East, along with the West Palace create a powerful auspicious prosperity matrix.

North West	North	North East
6	1	8
West		East
7 _____ *Direct Spirit*	5 ➤	3 *Indirect Spirit*
South West	South	South East
2	9	4

The ideal is to have water in front of the Indirect Spirit or Ling Shen Palace—it promotes prosperity throughout the entire building.

- All placements should be in harmony with the Flying Stars of the Palace of Water Placement. Do not place water where there is an untimely Water Star in the Indirect Spirit Palace.

- No water should be placed in the Direct Spirit Palace for Cycle Seven.

The following table lists the direct and indirect palaces for each cycle and their proper forms. The Indirect Spirit Palace is called "Ling Shen."

The Primary Fortune Palace is Southwest for all buildings in Cycle Eight (2004–2023).

Direct and Indirect Palaces

Number	Twenty-Year Cycle	Direct Spirit Palace	Indirect Spirit Palace
1	1864–1883	North Mountain	South Water
2	1884–1903	South West Mountain	North East Water
3	1904–1923	East Mountain	West Water
4	1924–1943	South East Mountain	North West Water
5	1944–1963	1st 10 years South West Mountain 2nd 10 years North East Mountain	1st 10 years North East Water 2nd 10 years South West Water
6	1964–1983	North West Mountain	South East Water
7	1984–2003	West Mountain	East Water
8	2004–2023	North East Mountain	South West Water
9	2024–2043	South Mountain	North Water

- No water in the Direct Spirit Palace

- No water with Untimely Water Stars

This Flying Star Feng Shui method is applicable in all nine cycles.

The influence of this palace extends throughout the entire building, not just in one palace and for those spending time in that one palace.

Second Direct Spirit Palace

Zhao Shen Palace

A Second Fortunate Palace exists for each twenty-year cycle. Placement of water in this palace promotes prosperity and wealth. It is most effective to place water outside the building, near timely or safe stars. Avoid placing water near untimely stars. Second Fortunate Palace is East for all buildings during Cycle Eight.

This method is based on the trigram relationships of the He Tu diagram and Later Heaven Ba Gua. Below is the He Tu diagram.

He Tu Diagram

	South Fire 4, 9	
East Wood 3, 8	Center Earth	West Metal 2, 7
	North Water 1, 6	

Examples 1 and 2 explain the formula.

Example 1
For the year 1935, the Twenty-Year Construction Cycle is Four. In the
He Tu diagram, Four is paired with Nine; the location of Nine in the
Later Heaven Ba Gua is the South Palace (see below). South is the
Secondary Fortunate Palace for Cycle Four.

Example 2
For the years 1984-2003, the cycle is Seven, which is paired with Two in
He Tu diagram; the palace containing Two in the Later Heaven Ba Gua
is South West. South West is the Secondary Fortunate Palace for Cycle
Seven (see the following Ba Gua).

Later Heaven Ba Gua

North West	North	North East
6	1	8
West		East
7	5	3
South West	South	South East
2	9	4

Second Spirit Palace Table

Number	Twenty-Year Cycle	Second Direct Spirit Palace
1	1864–1883	North West
2	1884–1903	West
3	1904–1923	North East
4	1924–1943	South
5	1944–1963	1st Ten years: West 2nd Ten years: East
6	1964–1983	North
7	1984–2003	South West
8	2004–2023	East
9	2024–2043	South East

- No water with Untimely Water Stars.

- This Flying Star Feng Shui method is applicable in all nine cycles.

Note:

For period Seven, East and Southwest are the Primary and Secondary Fortunate Palaces. For period Eight, they are Southwest for Primary and East for Secondary Fortunate Palaces. For both cycles, water can be placed in these directions for different reasons.

Sum to Ten Chart

There are Flying Stars Feng Shui charts that are very favorable based on special Nine Stars distribution throughout each palace. In one type, the total value of the Time Star in each palace is added to either the Water or Mountain Star and equals ten. The following example illustrates this special chart.

Example
1904–1923
Sitting or Sitting-Mountain Position: South 2

SE	S	SW
8 7 2	3 3 7 *sitting*	1 5 9
9 6 1	7 8 3	5 1 5
4 2 6	2 4 8 Facing	6 9 4

NE	N	NW

Each palace has a combination of two stars that equal ten. One Star must be the Time Star and the other can be the Mountain or Water Star. The particular star that sums to ten is the special star combination, and its related area of life has the potential for great good fortunate. For example, in the South East, the Mountain Star combines with the Time Star, promoting health and fertility. Every palace must sum to ten to fulfill this special chart.

This chart promotes the smooth flow of energy through every palace in the building, creating auspicious health, relationships and fertility. Proper forms must be present for this chart to be activated. The following lists proper forms:

1. The proper forms must be located near Timely Stars, water near the Timely Water Star and mountain near the Timely Mountain Star.

2. The building must be a complete square or rectangle; missing portions are not allowed for this special chart to be activated. This is a rigid traditional requirement, although success has been found in modern building structures too.

    All Sum to Ten charts are listed in the Flying Stars charts in the appendix.

Parent String

Fu Mu San Gua

1,4,7   2,5,8   3,6,9   Flying Stars Charts

Parent String is a special Flying Stars Feng Shui chart whose star pattern is 1,4,7 or 2,5,8 or 3,6,9 in each palace; this star formation generates great fortune and luck—the influence is so strong it overrides unfortunate charts. This energy pattern is based on the cycle of 180 years, which can be segmented into three cycles of sixty years. This formation has one star from each sixty-year cycle contained in each palace. See the cycle of twenty years below.

Cycle	Cycle	Years
Upper	1	1864–1883
	2	1884–1903
	3	1904–1923
Middle	4	1924–1943
	5	1944–1963
	6	1964–1983
Lower	7	1984–2003
	8	2004–2023
	9	2024–2043

Example: Construction Year 1965, Sitting-Mountain: North East 1

SE	S	SW
8 2 5	4 7 1	6 9 3 *Facing Palace*
7 1 4	9 3 6	2 5 8
3 6 9 *Sitting Palace*	5 8 2	1 4 7
NE	N	NW

When proper forms are present, this is a very favorable chart. This 1,4,7 and 2,5,8 and 3,6,9-style house transforms the unfavorable aspects of stars and promotes great luck and prosperity.

Pearl String

Lin Chu San Pan Kua

Pearl String is when stars flow in a sequential order in each palace, for example, when each palace flows in the following patterns: 1,2,3 4,5,6 7,8,9, in any order.

This chart, like all charts, needs the proper forms to activate timely stars. Traditionally, this style of building generates enormous prosperity, but lasts only for the twenty-year cycle in which it was built. For example, a building built in Cycle Seven will have this potential good fortune for 1984–2003. If the forms change to activate the new timely stars in new cycles, the favorable qualities can be extended.

This Qi distribution can flow from the Mountain, Time and Water Stars, promoting wealth, or from the Water, Time and Mountain Stars, promoting favorable health and relationships.

Fan Fu Yin

Inverse and Hidden Siren

This classic Flying Stars chart occurs when the Center Palace contains a Five Star in the Mountain or Water Star position.

- The Inverse Siren, or Fan Yin, is when the Five Star flies or floats downward or is in a yin pattern.

- The Hidden Siren, or Fu Yin, is when the Five Star flies or floats upward or is in a yang pattern.

If proper forms are present, these structures are neutralized; if not, these buildings will generate health, relationship or wealth problems. Creating proper forms for the four styles of buildings—for example, favorable for people and wealth, unfavorable for people and wealth, favorable for people and unfavorable for wealth and favorable for wealth and unfavorable for people—provides the proper harmony to remedy this condition.

He Tu Castle Gate

He Tu Castle Gate is a simple but potent method to increase prosperity. The method is listed below.

1. Locate the Facing Gua (Mountain) with a compass and identify it in column 1.

2. Place water in column two.

Later Heaven Gua Method

Building Facing Position	Place Water Here
North East Gen 8	East Zhen 3
East Zhen 3	North East Gen 8
South East Xun 4	South Li 9
South Li 9	South East Xun 4
South West Kun 2	West Dui 7
West Dui 7	South West Kun 2
North West Qian 6	North Kan 1
North Kan 1	North West Qian 6

This method is based on direction, not time—it does not change with new cycles of time.

Castle Gate

Castle Gate can promote prosperity in all areas of life.

•   This method is based on the Facing Gua of the building.

•   Use the Cycle Eight now.

•   Locate the Facing Mountain of the building in column one.
•   The water opportunities are found in column two.

Because the energies of nature move in transformations, Cycle Eight is exerting its influence now, in year 2003, Cycle Seven is declining. Use Cycle Eight now to capture the energy of the Timely Eight Star that is entering.

A traditional method for the Castle Gate is to surround three sides of a building and to leave an opening at the designated Castle Gate Mountain—it is at this mountain direction that water exists or is created. In modern living spaces we can make the real or virtual water placements inside the building.

Castle Gate for cycle Eight

Facing Mountain	Castle Gate Water Opportunities (Period 8)
N 1	SE 1, NE 1 (No Water NE)
N 2	SW 2, NW 2
N 3	SW 3, NW 3
NE 1	East 1 North 1,
NE 2	West 2, South 2
NE 3	West 3, South 3
E 1	NW 1, NE 1 (No Water NE)
E 2	SW 2, SE 2
E 3	SW 3, SE 3
SE 1	N 1, W 1
SE 2	S 2, W 2
SE 3	S 3, W 3
S 1	SW 1, NW 1
S 2	SE 2, NE 2 (No Water in NE)
S 3	SE 3, NE 3 (No Water in NE)
SW 1	N 1, E 1
SW 2	S 2, W 2
SW 3	S 3, W 3
W 1	SW 1, SE 1
W 2	NW 2, NE 2 (No Water in NE)
W 3	NW 3, NE 3 (No Water in NE)
NW 1	E 1, N 1
NW 2	W 2, S 2
NW 3	W 3, S 3

- No Water in the Direct Spirit Palace (Period 7 is West, Period 8 is NE)
- No Water with Untimely Stars

Water and Mountain Fan Gua

Five Ghosts Carry Money Opportunities

The classic Water and Mountain Fan Gua is a powerful method of promoting prosperity. This method has two parts, water and mountain. I have created tables that contain the completed method. If one of the methods exists or can be created, it is very favorable. If both of the conditions exist or can be created, you will have met the criterion of "Five Ghosts Carry Money," a most auspicious and prosperous condition, one of the most powerful Feng Shui methods for prosperity.

The method:

1. Find the *Facing Gua* (Mountain) in column one.

2. Place water in column two (Water Fan Gua).

3. A window or door in column three is Mountain Fan Gua.

4. When a building has both Mountain and Water Fan Gua it is "Five Ghost Carry Money", a very auspicious condition promoting prosperity and transcends Flying Stars Feng Shui.

Water and Mountain Fan Gua Table

Column 1	Column 2	Column 3
Mountain	Water Fan Gua Incoming Water Placement Here	Mountain Fan Gua Windows or Doors Located Here
N1	N 3 or SW 3 or N 2 or SE 1	N 1, NE 3, S 2, NW 1
N2	N 1 or NE 3 or S 2 or NW 1	NE 2, S 1
N3	N 1 or NE 3 or S 2 or NW 1	N 3, SW 3, N 2, SE 1
NE 1	NE 2 or S 1	SW 2, E 3
NE 2	S 3 or SE 3 or W 2 or NE 1	W 1, NW 3, E 2, SW 1
NE 3	N 3 or SW 3 or N 2 or SE 1	S 3, SE 3, W 2, NE 1
E 1	SW 2 or E 3	SW 2, E 3
E 2	SE 2 or W 3	N 3, SW 3, N 2, SE 1
E 3	NW 2 or E 1	NW 2, E 1
SE 1	N 1 or NE 3 or S 2 or NW 1	NE 2, S 1
SE 2	W 1 or NW 3 or E 2 or SW 1	SE 2, W 3
SE 3	NE 2 or S 1	SW 2, E 3
S 1	S 3 or SE 3 or W 2 or NE 1	NE 2, S 1
S 2	N 3 or SW 3 or N 2 or SE 1	S 3, SE 3, W 2, NE 1
S 3	NE 2 or S 1	S 3, SE 3, W 2, NE 1
SW 1	SE 2 or W 3	N 3, SW 3, N 2, SE 1
SW 2	NW 2 or E 1	N 1, NE 3, S 2, NW 1
SW 3	N 1 or NE 3 or S 2 or NW 1	NE 2, S 1
W 1	SE 2 or W 3	SE 2, W 3
W 2	NE 2 or S 1	SW 2, E 3
W 3	W 1 or NW 3 or E 2 or SW 1	W 1, NW 3, E 2, SW 1
NW 1	N 3 or SW 3 or N 2 or SE 1	S 3, SE 3, W 2, NE 1
NW 2	SW 2 or E 3	NW 2, E 1
NW 3	SE 2 or W 3	N 3, SW 3, N 2, SE 1

Annual Flying Stars

In addition to Mountain and Water Stars, Annual Flying Stars have a strong influence in Feng Shui. These stars are easy to calculate because they always float in ascending sequence. The following is a formula to determine Annual Flying Stars.

1. Select a year, for example, 1998.

2. Sum all digits in the year. $1 + 9 + 9 + 8 = 27$. The total is 27.

3. Sum the total again if it is greater than 9.
    $2 + 7 = 9$

4. Subtract the total in step 3 from 11.
    $11 - 9 = 2$

5. Two is the Annual Flying Stars for year 1998.

The table below lists Annual Flying Stars for years 2000–2010:

Annual Flying Stars

Star	Year
9	2000
8	2001
7	2002
6	2003
5	2004
4	2005
3	2006
2	2007
1	2008
9	2009
8	2010
7	2011

Floating Annual Flying Stars

Annual Stars are floated in ascending order. The Annual Star is placed in the Center Palace and floats in the following sequence: Center, North West, West, North East, South, North, South West, East and South East. See the following example:

Year 2002
Annual Flying Stars is 7.

SE	S	SW
6	2	4
5	7	9
1	3	8

| NE | N | NW |

For Feng Shui purposes, the New Year begins on February 4 or February 5. (If you need to know the exact day, feel free to contact the author.)

Annual Flying Stars affect Water, Mountain and Time Stars. As with all stars, determine their timeliness and evaluate the meanings they have individually and in combination with the Time, Mountain and Water Stars in each palace. If the Annual Star is unfavorable, use the Five-Element system as a remedy. It is vital to review all forms, including exterior and interior ones, and their influence on timely and untimely stars.

The table below lists the Annual Flying Stars for years 2003—2011:

Annual Flying Stars

Palace	2003	2004	2005	2006	2007	2008	2009	2010	2011
Center	6	5	4	3	2	1	9	8	7
North West	7	6	5	4	3	2	1	9	8
West	8	7	6	5	4	3	2	1	9
North East	9	8	7	6	5	4	3	2	1
South	1	9	8	7	6	5	4	3	2
North	2	1	9	8	7	6	5	4	3
South West	3	2	1	9	8	7	6	5	4
East	4	3	2	1	9	8	7	6	5
South East	5	4	3	2	1	9	8	7	6

Locate the year in the top row and place the star in the adjacent palace.

Monthly Flying Stars

Water, Mountain and Construction/Time Stars are the most influential stars, followed by Annual and Monthly Flying Stars. These last two stars must be evaluated to obtain a complete understanding of a living environment, as they are often a hidden cause of unfavorable and favorable activities. The Annual and Monthly Stars can combine with each other and with Mountain, Water or Time Stars.

Method:
Locate the Chinese Animal for the year in question in the top row of the table below and identify the month in question. The star in the box that intersects the Year Animal and Month is the Month Star.

Monthly Flying Stars

Month	Year of Rat, Rabbit, Horse, Cock	Year of Ox, Dragon, Sheep, Dog	Year of Tiger, Snake, Monkey, Pig
February 5	8	5	2
March 6	7	4	1
April 5	6	3	9
May 6	5	2	8
June 6	4	1	7
July 7	3	9	6
August 8	2	8	5
September 8	1	7	4
October 8	9	6	3
November 7	8	5	2
December 7	7	4	1
January 6	6	3	9

The beginning of the month can vary by a day. Feel free to contact the author to find the exact day for any month and year.

Luo Pan and Chinese Zodiac Animals

The Luo Pan compass contains the twelve branches or Chinese zodiac animals. Basic Four Pillars of Destiny (Chinese Astrology) knowledge reveals that opposite branches or animals clash with each other, creating disharmonies. These relationships are also applied to Feng Shui. Below are the 12-Chinese Zodiac animals.

Chinese Zodiac Animals & Luo Pan Degrees

	Snake 135-165	Horse 165-195	Sheep 195-225	
Dragon 105-135				Monkey 225-255
Rabbit 75-105				Cock 255-285
Tiger 45-75				Dog 285-315
	Ox 15-45	Rat 345-15	Pig 315-345	

Note the opposite pairs:

- Horse and Rat
- Ox and Sheep
- Tiger and Monkey
- Rabbit and Rooster
- Dragon and Dog
- Snake and Pig

It is very unfavorable to select a building with a facing mountain that is the opposite branch as your birth year. For example, a person born in the year of the snake should not live a building that faces the pig mountain. These are clash combinations which will cause people to argue, bicker, clash, and create and attract disharmonies. Avoid these situations.

Another application of the Chinese zodiac animals and the Luo Pan is to attract romance. This method is called "Peach Blossom." The following tables list the relevant information.

Each branch-animal is thirty degrees.

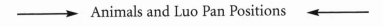 Animals and Luo Pan Positions

Luo Pan Position	Luo Pan Position
Pig 315-345	Snake 135-165
Rat 345-15	Horse 165-195
Ox 15-45	Sheep 195-225
Tiger 45-75	Monkey 225-285
Rabbit 75-105	Cock 255-285
Dragon 105-135	Dog 285-315

Application:

1.   Peach Blossom relates to romance.

•   If the proper geographical area is activated then a person with the associated Chinese animal will attract Romance in their life.

•   The way to activate an area is to place beautiful flowers in the geographical area; keep the water and flowers fresh and clean.

•   If flowers are placed in the Horse location (165-195 degrees on the Luo Pan), people born in the year of the Rooster, Ox and Snake will attract romance.

•   Some practitioners use the year branch and others use the day branch-animal—you can try both.

Animal Sign	Peach Blossom
Rat, Dragon or Monkey	Rooster
Tiger, Horse or Dog	Rabbit
Rabbit, Sheep or Pig	Rat
Ox, Snake or Cock	Horse

Grand Duke
Tai Sui

The planet Jupiter is referred to as the "Grand Duke." It circles the Sun every twelve years, creating an energetic influence that permeates the planet Earth. Each year this energy encompasses a fifteen-degree area on a compass and exerts a potentially unfavorable influence. Basically, one should not face this direction or perform renovations or remodeling in this area; this area should remain inactive. These locations cover fifteen degrees of the Luo Pan Compass and relate directly to the Chinese annual zodiac animals. The following table lists locations for the Grand Duke.

Year	Grand Duke Tai Sui	Luo Pan Position
2001	Snake Yang Fire	142.5-157.5 degrees SE 3
2002	Horse Yin Fire	172.5-187.5 degrees South 2
2003	Sheep Yin Earth	202.5-217.5 degrees SW 1
2004	Monkey Yang Metal	232.5-247.5 degrees SW 3
2005	Cock Yin Metal	262.5-277.5 degrees W 2
2006	Dog Yang Earth	292.5-307.5 degrees NW 1
2007	Pig Yang Water	315-345 degrees NW 3
2008	Rat Yin Water	352.5-7.5 degrees N 2
2009	Ox Yin Water	22.5-37.5 degrees NE 1

Applications:

1. Many practitioners believe this is a critical aspect of Feng Shui and must be managed properly. Traditional recommendations include not facing this direction or disturbing this area (for instance, performing renovations, reconstruction, etc.) during the year.

2. Some believe the influence of the Grand Duke is based on Chinese Astrology or the Four Pillars. If the year animal/branch is favorable to your astrology chart then that area can be favorable to you or the Grand Duke's negative influence will be decreased. If the year animal/branch is unfavorable to your Four Pillars/Astrology Chart, it will be unfavorable.

3. The Grand Duke's element for the year (for example, fire for year 2002/Horse) will have an influence on the Flying Stars in the related palace of the Grand Duke. If fire is unfavorable to stars in its related palace, it will exacerbate the star(s).

4. Convention is to avoid facing and disturbing this area.

Three Killings

Sarm Sart

Year	Element Frame	Location of Three Killings
Rat, Monkey, Dragon	Water	South
Rabbit, Sheep. Pig	Wood	West
Cock, Ox, Snake	Metal	East
Horse, Dog, Tiger	Fire	North

This is the trinity, or the element-frame relationships, found in Four Pillars Astrology. The location of the Three Killings is the element that opposes the Grand Duke Year Element.

Applications:

- You can face this direction, but avoid renovations or repairs in this area, for they will bring misfortune.

- You may face this area, but do not have it to your back.

Evil Lines

These lines are located at the beginning and end of the eight cardinal directions. There are numerous applications of these evil lines. Most practitioners believe that if a building's Facing and Sitting direction falls on these lines, there will be very unfavorable consequences in all aspects of life, and most believe the lines extend 1.5 degrees to each side of the line. Generally avoid these homes. Basically, these buildings are influenced by two major guas or directions, creating confusion and a lack of stability and clarity.

Evil Lines	Locations
22.5	North 3/North East 1
67.5	North East 3/East 1
112.5	East 3/South East 1
157.5	South East 3/South 1
202.5	South 3/South West 1
247.5	South West 3/West 1
292.5	West 3/North West 1
337.5	North West 3/ North 1

Steps for Practicing Flying Stars Feng Shui

- Determine the orientation of the building, or its Facing and Sitting locations.

- Identify which of the four types of charts the structure represents and if the current cycle is the Twenty-Year Construction Period; if so, use the recommended form placements for the original twenty-year cycle.

- If a building is out of its Twenty-Year Construction Cycle, make form corrections based on the current cycle of timeliness; also, look at other Flying Star methods to promote prosperity, auspicious relationships and health. For example, focus on the Primary and Secondary Palaces and at supporting timely stars with proper forms.

- The Facing and Sitting Palaces are the most influential on the entire building and should have priority when you are evaluating and applying remedies. If these are favorable, the building will be favorable, unless there is something very unfavorable elsewhere.

- Check to see if the building is locked; if so, make the proper remedies.

- Evaluate exterior forms and their individual energies—are they favorable or unfavorable?

- Identify timely stars and exterior and interior forms next to them.

- Check to see whether the building is a special chart formation.

- Identify favorable stars in the structure and use proper forms and Five-Element remedies to activate them.

- Identify special star combinations and use forms and the Five Elements to activate them.

- Identify unfavorable stars and use forms and the Five Elements as remedies.

- Evaluate each palace's original Five-Element nature and its influence on Mountain and Water Stars—these are minor influences, for example, the South is Fire and West is Metal.

- Evaluate each palace's Twenty-Year Construction Star and its influence on Sitting and Facing Stars—these are minor influences. These stars are the lower middle stars in each palace.

- Evaluate Annual and Monthly Stars and their influences in the palaces they enter—they can be activators.

- Review Interior Design Forms and their influences.

- Water and mountains in the environment and inside the building are vibrant energy sources—they can be real or virtual. They are powerful in all systems of Feng Shui and particularly potent in Flying Stars Feng Shui. These forms are most potent as activators of Flying Stars, generally more potent than Five-Element remedies added in palaces to harmonize stars.

•   Remember, the front door, bedroom, office and areas where one spends time are most important in Feng Shui.

•   Always harmonize the Untimely Five Star, whether it is in the original chart or in annual or monthly cycles. A grandfather clock or perpetual sounding metal chimes are effective remedies.

•   Use transcendental items to enhance one's environment. For example, if the Three Star is untimely and in the bedroom, place a picture that reflects beautiful communication skills to assist in your efforts in promoting this quality.

•   Use mirrors to move Qi and expand the area. Another unique technique is to place a mirror in an area with unfavorable stars, with it facing an area that has favorable stars, to draw the Sheng Qi into the area.

•   If one is in an important area that has unfavorable stars and a door, check to see the area in which the door is located—is it in a different palace with favorable stars? If so, this Sheng Qi enters the area, creating a favorable influence. If you can move the door to an area with favorable stars its influence can transcend unfavorable stars in the area. The door draws in favorable Qi into the area.

- The placement of water is a critical aspect of Feng Shui. Great care is necessary and special knowledge is required for all water placements. When in doubt, do not use water and consult a professional trained in the art of Water Dragon Placement formulas. Feel free to contact me for this type of analysis.

Feng Shui Example

Example 1
Analysis is for Cycle 7
Date of consultation: February 2, 2000
House constructed in 1980 (Cycle Six)
Mountain-Sitting position: North West Three
Water-Facing Position: South East Three

Facing

SE 8 4 5 Living Room	S 3 9 1 Living Room	SW 1 2 3 Living Room
E 9 3 4 Kitchen	<u>7</u> 5 <u>6</u> Living Room	W 5 7 8 Bedroom
NE 4 8 9 Entrance	N 2 1 2 Bathroom	NW <u>6 6</u> 7 Hallway

Sitting

177

- This structure is "locked" for health and fertility from 1984 to 2003. This is reflected by the Seven Star being located in the Sitting position in the Center Palace. Select the best remedy for a locked condition. Implement one of the methods to release a locked building.

- This is a Double Stars meeting in the Sitting Palace Structure. This chart is most vibrant during Cycle Six, years 1964–1983. During Cycle Seven, the qualities of this Double Stars meeting at the Sitting Palace special chart no longer exist. If one had a mountain and water form to activate the double stars in the sitting palace (NW) during Cycle Six, they would not create problems for at least sixty years after Cycle Six, because star six reverts to its original nature in Cycle Seven and is safe in cycles Eight and Nine.

- Because the house was built in the previous twenty-year cycle, the Double Sitting opportunity is not in its most vibrant period.

  The East contains Star Three. It is untimely for Cycle Seven. Do not activate this untimely star, even though it is the Ling Shen Palace.

- The entrance in the North East is 4,8. Four Star is wood and Controls Eight Star, earth. Eight Star is timely and good for fame and fortune. Four Star is usable. Fame, fortune and career is dominated and repressed according to the Five Elements—this combination may create emotional difficulties, isolation and obstacles for children. Add fire to break the domination, allowing fame, fortune and prosperity to manifest while eliminating unfavorable influences resulting from wood controlling earth.

- A bedroom is in the West and contains stars 5 and 7. Seven is the timely star and is excellent for wealth. This combination may create mouth problems and food poisoning if no Five-Element remedy is introduced—the negative Five Star must be reduced and not activated. Add metal in the bedroom. Additionally, the unfavorable Earth Star is the parent of Timely Metal Seven Star and strengthens this favorable star.

  It is important not to activate the unfavorable Five Star with interior or exterior forms.

- South East is 8,4. See the *entrance evaluation* above for the meaning of each star and the 4,8 combination. Add fire to break the domination of Four Wood Star on Eight Earth Star. Eight Star is Timely and Four Star is usable.

  A mountain form is auspicious for the Timely Eight Star.

- In the South, Three Wood Star is Untimely and generates gossip, arguments and lawsuits and Nine Fire Star is Future Timely and favorable. This combination generates wealth and fame. Add fire to reduce the unfavorable Three Wood Star and its negative influences.

  One may want to place a picture or object that reflects good communications as a way to focus on transcending the unfavorable Star Three during Cycle Seven.

- In the South West, unfavorable Two Earth Star controls the usable One Water Star. Water relates to the kidneys, and this 1,2 Star combination can cause health and fertility problems—

especially kidney, blood and ear problems—as well as spousal difficulty, female domination and abdominal pain. Add metal to break the domination and reduce the unfavorable Two Earth Star and strengthen Water One Star.

It is critical not to activate the unfavorable Two Star.

- He Tu Castle Gate method for this building is South 3 and is not favorable for Water placement because of the unfavorable Three Star.

- The Castle locations for this building are West 3 and South 3. During Cycle Seven we avoid water in the West; the South contains Stars 3 and 9. I recommend virtual water in this palace, as real water may activate the unfavorable three star during period seven.

- Water Fan Gua can be placed in the North East 2 area (Stars 4 and 8); the kitchen in the East is Mountain Fan Gua and has windows. Both of these conditions are met, creating "Five Ghosts Carry Money," a most auspicious influence.

Appendix

Flying Stars Feng Shui Charts

Flying Stars Feng Shui charts in this Appendix are organized with South at the top and North at the bottom. The following example illustrates the structure.

South East	South	South West
East		West
North East	North	North West

One reason charts are traditionally presented this way is that in ancient times, sunlight was of highest value. The North represents Yin, water and darkness and South Yang, fire and light. The sun rises in the East and represents Spring, wood and sunlight, and peaks in the South, which is the fire element. Fire, being Yang, is positioned at the top. Yang ascends. North, representing darkness, is positioned at the bottom. Yin descends.

Flying Star chart: Cycle 1

	S	
7 4 / 9	2 9 / 5	9 2 / 7
E 8 3 / 8	6 5 / 1	W 4 7 / 3
3 8 / 4	N 1 1 / 6	5 6 / 2

Sitting: North 1
Double Sitting
Hidden Siren

	S	
5 6 / 9	1 1 / 5	3 8 / 7
E 4 7 / 8	6 5 / 1	W 8 3 / 3
9 2 / 4	N 2 9 / 6	7 4 / 2

Sitting: North 2
Double Facing
Inverse Siren

	S	
5 6 / 9	1 1 / 5	3 8 / 7
E 4 7 / 8	6 5 / 1	W 8 3 / 3
9 2 / 4	N 2 9 / 6	7 4 / 2

Sitting: North 3
Double Facing
Inverse Siren

	S	
5 6 / 9	9 2 / 5	7 4 / 7
E 6 5 / 8	4 7 / 1	W 2 9 / 3
1 1 / 4	N 8 3 / 6	3 8 / 2

Sitting: North East 1
Double Sitting

	S	
3 8 / 9	8 3 / 5	1 1 / 7
E 2 9 / 8	4 7 / 1	W 6 5 / 3
7 4 / 4	N 9 2 / 6	5 6 / 2

Sitting: North East 2
Double Facing

	S	
3 8 / 9	8 3 / 5	1 1 / 7
E 2 9 / 8	4 7 / 1	W 6 5 / 3
7 4 / 4	N 9 2 / 6	5 6 / 2

Sitting: North East 2
Double Facing

	S	
9 2 / 9	4 7 / 5	2 9 / 7
E 1 1 / 8	8 3 / 1	W 6 5 / 3
5 6 / 4	N 3 8 / 6	7 4 / 2

Sitting: East 1
Double Sitting
Locked period eight

	S	
7 4 / 9	3 8 / 5	5 6 / 7
E 6 5 / 8	8 3 / 1	W 1 1 / 3
2 9 / 4	N 4 7 / 6	9 2 / 2

Sitting: East 2
Double Facing
Locked period eight

	S	
7 4 / 9	3 8 / 5	5 6 / 7
E 6 5 / 8	8 3 / 1	W 1 1 / 3
2 9 / 4	N 4 7 / 6	9 2 / 2

Sitting: East 3
Double Facing
Locked period eight

	S	
8 3 / 9	4 7 / 5	6 5 / 7
E 7 4 / 8	9 2 / 1	W 2 9 / 3
3 8 / 4	N 5 6 / 6	1 1 / 2

Sitting: South East 1
Double Facing

	S	
1 1 / 9	5 6 / 5	3 8 / 7
E 2 9 / 8	9 2 / 1	W 7 4 / 3
6 5 / 4	N 4 7 / 6	8 3 / 2

Sitting: South East 2
Double Sitting
Sum to 10

	S	
1 1 / 9	5 6 / 5	3 8 / 7
E 2 9 / 8	9 2 / 1	W 7 4 / 3
6 5 / 4	N 4 7 / 6	8 3 / 2

Sitting: South East 3
Double Sitting
Sum to 10

Flying Star chart: Cycle 1

Sitting: South 1

	S	
4 7 / 9	9 2 / 5	2 9 / 7
E 3 8 / 8	5 6 / 1	7 4 / 3 W
8 3 / 4	N 1 1 / 6	6 5 / 2

Sitting: South 1
Double Facing
Hidden Siren

Sitting: South 2

	S	
6 5 / 9	1 1 / 5	8 3 / 7
E 7 4 / 8	5 6 / 1	3 8 / 3 W
2 9 / 4	N 9 2 / 6	4 7 / 2

Sitting: South 2
Double Sitting
Inverse Siren

Sitting: South 3

	S	
6 5 / 9	1 1 / 5	8 3 / 7
E 7 4 / 8	5 6 / 1	3 8 / 3 W
2 9 / 4	N 9 2 / 6	4 7 / 2

Sitting: South 3
Double Sitting
Inverse Siren

Sitting: South West 1

	S	
6 5 / 9	2 9 / 5	4 7 / 7
E 5 6 / 8	7 4 / 1	9 2 / 3 W
1 1 / 4	N 3 8 / 6	8 3 / 2

Sitting: South West 1
Double Facing

Sitting: South West 2

	S	
8 3 / 9	3 8 / 5	1 1 / 7
E 9 2 / 8	7 4 / 1	5 6 / 3 W
4 7 / 4	N 2 9 / 6	6 5 / 2

Sitting: South West 2
Double Sitting

Sitting: South West 3

	S	
8 3 / 9	3 8 / 5	1 1 / 7
E 9 2 / 8	7 4 / 1	5 6 / 3 W
4 7 / 4	N 2 9 / 6	6 5 / 2

Sitting: South West 3
Double Sitting

Sitting: West 1

	S	
2 9 / 9	7 4 / 5	9 2 / 7
E 1 1 / 8	3 8 / 1	5 6 / 3 W
6 5 / 4	N 8 3 / 6	4 7 / 2

Sitting: West 1
Double Facing
Locked period eight

Sitting: West 2

	S	
4 7 / 9	8 3 / 5	6 5 / 7
E 5 6 / 8	3 8 / 1	1 1 / 3 W
9 2 / 4	N 7 4 / 6	2 9 / 2

Sitting: West 2
Double Sitting
Locked period eight

Sitting: West 3

	S	
4 7 / 9	8 3 / 5	6 5 / 7
E 5 6 / 8	3 8 / 1	1 1 / 3 W
9 2 / 4	N 7 4 / 6	2 9 / 2

Sitting: West 3
Double Sitting
Locked period eight

Sitting: North West 1

	S	
3 8 / 9	7 4 / 5	5 6 / 7
E 4 7 / 8	2 9 / 1	9 2 / 3 W
8 3 / 4	N 6 5 / 6	1 1 / 2

Sitting: North West 1
Double Sitting

Sitting: North West 2

	S	
1 1 / 9	6 5 / 5	8 3 / 7
E 9 2 / 8	2 9 / 1	4 7 / 3 W
5 6 / 4	N 7 4 / 6	3 8 / 2

Sitting: North West 2
Double Facing
Sum to 10

Sitting: North West 3

	S	
1 1 / 9	6 5 / 5	8 3 / 7
E 9 2 / 8	2 9 / 1	4 7 / 3 W
5 6 / 4	N 7 4 / 6	3 8 / 2

Sitting: North West 3
Double Facing
Sum to 10

Flying Star chart: Cycle 2

	S	
6 7 1	2 2 6	4 9 8
E 5 8 9	7 6 2	**W** 9 4 4
1 3 5	**N** 3 1 7	8 5 3

Sitting: North 1
Double Facing

	S	
8 5 1	3 1 6	1 3 8
E 9 4 9	7 6 2	**W** 5 8 4
4 9 5	**N** 2 2 7	6 7 3

Sitting: North 2
Double Sitting

	S	
8 5 1	3 1 6	1 3 8
E 9 4 9	7 6 2	**W** 5 8 4
4 9 5	**N** 2 2 7	6 7 3

Sitting: North 3
Double Sitting

	S	
6 9 1	1 4 6	8 2 8
E 7 1 9	5 8 2	**W** 3 6 4
2 5 5	**N** 9 3 7	4 7 3

Sitting: North East 1
Wang Shan
Sum to 10
Inverse Siren
Locked period eight

	S	
4 7 1	9 3 6	2 5 8
E 3 6 9	5 8 2	**W** 7 1 4
8 2 5	**N** 1 4 7	6 9 3

Sitting: North East 2
Shang Shan
Parent String
Hidden Siren
Locked period eight

	S	
4 7 1	9 3 6	2 5 8
E 3 6 9	5 8 2	**W** 7 1 4
8 2 5	**N** 1 4 7	6 9 3

Sitting: North East 3
Shang Shan
Parent String
Hidden Siren
Locked period eight

	S	
8 5 1	4 9 6	6 7 8
E 7 6 9	9 4 2	**W** 2 2 4
3 1 5	**N** 5 8 7	1 3 3

Sitting: East 1
Double Facing

	S	
1 3 1	5 8 6	3 1 8
E 2 2 9	9 4 2	**W** 7 6 4
6 7 5	**N** 4 9 7	8 5 3

Sitting: East 2
Double Sitting

	S	
1 3 1	5 8 6	3 1 8
E 2 2 9	9 4 2	**W** 7 6 4
6 7 5	**N** 4 9 7	8 5 3

Sitting: East 3
Double Sitting

	S	
9 2 1	5 7 6	7 9 8
E 8 1 9	1 3 2	**W** 3 5 4
4 6 5	**N** 6 8 7	2 4 3

Sitting: South East 1
Shan Shang
Pearl String

	S	
2 4 1	6 8 6	4 6 8
E 3 5 9	1 3 2	**W** 8 1 4
7 9 5	**N** 5 7 7	9 2 3

Sitting: South East 2
Wang Shan

	S	
2 4 1	6 8 6	4 6 8
E 3 5 9	1 3 2	**W** 8 1 4
7 9 5	**N** 5 7 7	9 2 3

Sitting: South East 3
Wang Shan

Flying Star chart: Cycle 2

Sitting: South 1
Double Sitting

	S	
7 6 / 1	2 2 / 6	9 4 / 8
E 8 5 / 9	6 7 / 2	W 4 9 / 4
3 1 / 5	N 1 3 / 7	5 8 / 3

Sitting: South 2
Double Facing

	S	
5 8 / 1	1 3 / 6	3 1 / 8
E 4 9 / 9	6 7 / 2	W 8 5 / 4
9 4 / 5	N 2 2 / 7	7 6 / 3

Sitting: South 3
Double Facing

	S	
5 8 / 1	1 3 / 6	3 1 / 8
E 4 9 / 9	6 7 / 2	W 8 5 / 4
9 4 / 5	N 2 2 / 7	7 6 / 3

Sitting: South West 1
Wang Shan
Sum to Ten
Inverse Siren
Locked period eight

	S	
9 6 / 1	4 1 / 6	2 8 / 8
E 1 7 / 9	8 5 / 2	W 6 3 / 4
5 2 / 5	N 3 9 / 7	7 4 / 3

Sitting: South West 2
Shang Shan
Parent String
Hidden Siren
Locked period eight

	S	
7 4 / 1	3 9 / 6	5 2 / 8
E 6 3 / 9	8 5 / 2	W 1 7 / 4
2 8 / 5	N 4 1 / 7	9 6 / 3

Sitting: South West 3
Shang Shan
Parent String
Hidden Siren
Locked period eight

	S	
7 4 / 1	3 9 / 6	5 2 / 8
E 6 3 / 9	8 5 / 2	W 1 7 / 4
2 8 / 5	N 4 1 / 7	9 6 / 3

Sitting: West 1
Double Sitting

	S	
5 8 / 1	9 4 / 6	7 6 / 8
E 6 7 / 9	4 9 / 2	W 2 2 / 4
1 3 / 5	N 8 5 / 7	3 1 / 3

Sitting: West 2
Double Facing

	S	
3 1 / 1	8 5 / 6	1 3 / 8
E 2 2 / 9	4 9 / 2	W 6 7 / 4
7 6 / 5	N 9 4 / 7	5 8 / 3

Sitting: West 3
Double Facing

	S	
3 1 / 1	8 5 / 6	1 3 / 8
E 2 2 / 9	4 9 / 2	W 6 7 / 4
7 6 / 5	N 9 4 / 7	5 8 / 3

Sitting: North West 1
Shang Shan
Pear String

	S	
2 9 / 1	7 5 / 6	9 7 / 8
E 1 8 / 9	3 1 / 2	W 5 3 / 4
6 4 / 5	N 8 6 / 7	4 2 / 3

Sitting: North West 2
Wang Shan

	S	
4 2 / 1	8 6 / 6	6 4 / 8
E 5 3 / 9	3 1 / 2	W 1 8 / 4
9 7 / 5	N 7 5 / 7	2 9 / 3

Sitting: North West 3
Wang Shan

	S	
4 2 / 1	8 6 / 6	6 4 / 8
E 5 3 / 9	3 1 / 2	W 1 8 / 4
9 7 / 5	N 7 5 / 7	2 9 / 3

Flying Star chart: Cycle 3

	S	
9 6 / 2	4 2 / 7	2 4 / 9
E 1 5 / 1	8 7 / 3	**W** 6 9 / 5
5 1 / 6	**N** 3 3 / 8	7 8 / 4

Sitting: North 1
Double Sitting
Locked period eight

	S	
7 8 / 2	3 3 / 7	5 1 / 9
E 6 9 / 1	8 7 / 3	**W** 1 5 / 5
2 4 / 6	**N** 4 2 / 8	9 6 / 4

Sitting: North 2
Double Facing
Locked period eight
Sum to Ten

	S	
7 8 / 2	3 3 / 7	5 1 / 9
E 6 9 / 1	8 7 / 3	**W** 1 5 / 5
2 4 / 6	**N** 4 2 / 8	9 6 / 4

Sitting: North 3
Double Facing
Locked period eight
Sum to Ten

	S	
7 8 / 2	2 4 / 7	9 6 / 9
E 8 7 / 1	6 9 / 3	**W** 4 2 / 5
3 3 / 6	**N** 1 5 / 8	5 1 / 4

Sitting: North East 1
Double Sitting

	S	
5 1 / 2	1 5 / 7	3 3 / 9
E 4 2 / 1	6 9 / 3	**W** 8 7 / 5
9 6 / 6	**N** 2 4 / 8	7 8 / 4

Sitting: North East 2
Double Facing

	S	
5 1 / 2	1 5 / 7	3 3 / 9
E 4 2 / 1	6 9 / 3	**W** 8 7 / 5
9 6 / 6	**N** 2 4 / 8	7 8 / 4

Sitting: North East 3
Double Facing

	S	
9 4 / 2	5 9 / 7	7 2 / 9
E 8 3 / 1	1 5 / 3	**W** 3 7 / 5
4 8 / 6	**N** 6 1 / 8	2 6 / 4

Sitting: East 1
Shang Shan
Hidden Siren

	S	
2 6 / 2	6 1 / 7	4 8 / 9
E 3 7 / 1	1 5 / 3	**W** 8 3 / 5
7 2 / 6	**N** 5 9 / 8	9 4 / 4

Sitting: East 2
Wang Shan
Inverse Siren

	S	
2 6 / 2	6 1 / 7	4 8 / 9
E 3 7 / 1	1 5 / 3	**W** 8 3 / 5
7 2 / 6	**N** 5 9 / 8	9 4 / 4

Sitting: East 3
Wang Shan
Inverse Siren

	S	
3 5 / 2	7 9 / 7	5 7 / 9
E 4 6 / 1	2 4 / 3	**W** 9 2 / 5
8 1 / 6	**N** 6 8 / 8	1 3 / 4

Sitting: South East 1
Wang Shan

	S	
1 3 / 2	6 8 / 7	8 1 / 9
E 9 2 / 1	2 4 / 3	**W** 4 6 / 5
5 7 / 6	**N** 7 9 / 8	3 5 / 4

Sitting: South East 2
Shang Shan
Pearl String

	S	
1 3 / 2	6 8 / 7	8 1 / 9
E 9 2 / 1	2 4 / 3	**W** 4 6 / 5
5 7 / 6	**N** 7 9 / 8	3 5 / 4

Sitting: South East 3
Shang Shan
Pearl String

Flying Star chart: Cycle 3

S		
6 9 2	**2 4 7**	4 2 9
E 5 1 1	7 8 3	**W** 9 6 5
	N 3 3 8	
1 5 6	3 3 8	8 7 4

Sitting: South 1
Double Facing
Locked period eight

S		
8 7 2	**3 3 7**	1 5 9
E 9 6 1	7 8 3	**W** 5 1 5
4 2 6	**N** 2 4 8	6 9 4

Sitting: South 2
Double Sitting
Sum to Ten
Locked period eight

S		
8 7 2	**3 3 7**	1 5 9
E 9 6 1	7 8 3	**W** 5 1 5
4 2 6	**N** 2 4 8	6 9 4

Sitting: South 3
Double Sitting
Sum to Ten
Locked period eight

S		
8 7 2	4 2 7	**6 9 9**
E 7 8 1	9 6 3	**W** 2 4 5
3 3 6	**N** 5 1 8	1 5 4

Sitting: South West 1
Double Facing

S		
1 5 2	5 1 7	**3 3 9**
E 2 4 1	9 6 3	**W** 7 8 5
6 9 6	**N** 4 2 8	8 7 4

Sitting: South West 2
Double Sitting

S		
1 5 2	5 1 7	**3 3 9**
E 2 4 1	9 6 3	**W** 7 8 5
6 9 6	**N** 4 2 8	8 7 4

Sitting: South West 3
Double Sitting

S		
4 9 2	9 5 7	2 7 9
E 3 8 1	5 1 3	**W** **7 3 5**
8 4 6	**N** 1 6 8	6 2 4

Sitting: West 1
Shang Shan
Hidden Siren

S		
6 2 2	1 6 7	8 4 9
E 7 3 1	5 1 3	**W** **3 8 5**
2 7 6	**N** 9 5 8	4 9 4

Sitting: West 2
Wang Shan
Inverse Siren

S		
6 2 2	1 6 7	8 4 9
E 7 3 1	5 1 3	**W** **3 8 5**
2 7 6	**N** 9 5 8	4 9 4

Sitting: West 3
Wang Shan
Inverse Siren

S		
5 3 2	9 7 7	7 5 9
E 6 4 1	4 2 3	**W** 2 9 5
1 8 6	**N** 8 6 8	**3 1 4**

Sitting: North West 1
Wang Shan

S		
3 1 2	8 6 7	1 8 9
E 2 9 1	4 2 3	**W** 6 4 5
7 5 6	**N** 9 7 8	**5 3 4**

Sitting: North West 2
Shang Shan
Pearl String

S		
3 1 2	8 6 7	1 8 9
E 2 9 1	4 2 3	**W** 6 4 5
7 5 6	**N** 9 7 8	**5 3 4**

Sitting: North West 3
Shang Shan
Pearl String

Flying Star chart: Cycle 4

	S	
8 9 / 3	4 4 / 8	6 2 / 1
E 7 1 / 2	9 8 / 4	**W** 2 6 / 6
3 5 / 7	**N** 5 3 / 9	1 7 / 5

Sitting: North 1
Double Facing
Locked period eight

	S	
1 7 / 3	5 3 / 8	3 5 / 1
E 2 6 / 2	9 8 / 4	**W** 7 1 / 6
6 2 / 7	**N** 4 4 / 9	8 9 / 5

Sitting: North 2
Double Sitting
Locked period eight

	S	
1 7 / 3	5 3 / 8	3 5 / 1
E 2 6 / 2	9 8 / 4	**W** 7 1 / 6
6 2 / 7	**N** 4 4 / 9	8 9 / 5

Sitting: North 3
Double Sitting
Locked period eight

	S	
6 9 / 3	2 5 / 8	4 7 / 1
E 5 8 / 2	7 1 / 4	**W** 9 3 / 6
1 4 / 7	**N** 3 6 / 9	8 2 / 5

Sitting: North East 1
Shang Shan
Parent String

	S	
8 2 / 3	3 6 / 8	1 4 / 1
E 9 3 / 2	7 1 / 4	**W** 5 8 / 6
4 7 / 7	**N** 2 5 / 9	6 9 / 5

Sitting: North East 2
Wang Shan

	S	
8 2 / 3	3 6 / 8	1 4 / 1
E 9 3 / 2	7 1 / 4	**W** 5 8 / 6
4 7 / 7	**N** 2 5 / 9	6 9 / 5

Sitting: North East 3
Wang Shan

	S	
3 7 / 3	7 2 / 8	5 9 / 1
E 4 8 / 2	2 6 / 4	**W** 9 4 / 6
8 3 / 7	**N** 6 1 / 9	1 5 / 5

Sitting: East 1
Wang Shan
Sum to Ten

	S	
1 5 / 3	6 1 / 8	8 3 / 1
E 9 4 / 2	2 6 / 4	**W** 4 8 / 6
5 9 / 7	**N** 7 2 / 9	3 7 / 5

Sitting: East 2
Shang Shan

	S	
1 5 / 3	6 1 / 8	8 3 / 1
E 9 4 / 2	2 6 / 4	**W** 4 8 / 6
5 9 / 7	**N** 7 2 / 9	3 7 / 5

Sitting: East 3
Shang Shan

	S	
2 6 / 3	7 1 / 8	9 8 / 1
E 1 7 / 2	3 5 / 4	**W** 5 3 / 6
6 2 / 7	**N** 8 9 / 9	4 4 / 5

Sitting: South East 1
Double Facing
Inverse Hidden

	S	
4 4 / 3	8 9 / 8	6 2 / 1
E 5 3 / 2	3 5 / 4	**W** 1 7 / 6
9 8 / 7	**N** 7 1 / 9	2 6 / 5

Sitting: South East 2
Double Sitting
Hidden Siren

	S	
4 4 / 3	8 9 / 8	6 2 / 1
E 5 3 / 2	3 5 / 4	**W** 1 7 / 6
9 8 / 7	**N** 7 1 / 9	2 6 / 5

Sitting: South East 3
Double Sitting
Hidden Siren

Flying Star chart: Cycle 4

	S	
9 8 / 3	4 4 / 8	2 6 / 1
E 1 7 / 2	8 9 / 4	W 6 2 / 6
5 3 / 7	N 3 5 / 9	7 1 / 5

Sitting: South 1
Double Sitting
Locked period eight

	S	
7 1 / 3	3 5 / 8	5 3 / 1
E 6 2 / 2	8 9 / 4	W 1 7 / 6
2 6 / 7	N 4 4 / 9	9 8 / 5

Sitting: South 2
Double Facing
Locked period eight

	S	
7 1 / 3	3 5 / 8	5 3 / 1
E 6 2 / 2	8 9 / 4	W 1 7 / 6
2 6 / 7	N 4 4 / 9	9 8 / 5

Sitting: South 3
Double Facing
Locked period eight

	S	
9 6 / 3	5 2 / 8	7 4 / 1
E 8 5 / 2	1 7 / 4	W 3 9 / 6
4 1 / 7	N 6 3 / 9	2 8 / 5

Sitting: South West 1
Shang Shan
Parent String

	S	
2 8 / 3	6 3 / 8	4 1 / 1
E 3 9 / 2	1 7 / 4	W 8 5 / 6
7 4 / 7	N 5 2 / 9	9 6 / 5

Sitting: South West 2
Wang Shan

	S	
2 8 / 3	6 3 / 8	4 1 / 1
E 3 9 / 2	1 7 / 4	W 8 5 / 6
7 4 / 7	N 5 2 / 9	9 6 / 5

Sitting: South West 3
Wang Shan

	S	
7 3 / 3	2 7 / 8	9 5 / 1
E 8 4 / 2	6 2 / 4	W 4 9 / 6
3 8 / 7	N 1 6 / 9	5 1 / 5

Sitting: West 1
Wang Shan
Sum to Ten

	S	
5 1 / 3	1 6 / 8	3 8 / 1
E 4 9 / 2	6 2 / 4	W 8 4 / 6
9 5 / 7	N 2 7 / 9	7 3 / 5

Sitting: West 2
Shang Shan

	S	
5 1 / 3	1 6 / 8	3 8 / 1
E 4 9 / 2	6 2 / 4	W 8 4 / 6
9 5 / 7	N 2 7 / 9	7 3 / 5

Sitting: West 3
Shang Shan

	S	
6 2 / 3	1 7 / 8	8 9 / 1
E 7 1 / 2	5 3 / 4	W 3 5 / 6
2 6 / 7	N 9 8 / 9	4 4 / 5

Sitting: North West 1
Double Sitting
Inverse Siren

	S	
4 4 / 3	9 8 / 8	2 6 / 1
E 3 5 / 2	5 3 / 4	W 7 1 / 6
8 9 / 7	N 1 7 / 9	6 2 / 5

Sitting: North West 2
Double Facing
Hidden Siren

	S	
4 4 / 3	9 8 / 8	2 6 / 1
E 3 5 / 2	5 3 / 4	W 7 1 / 6
8 9 / 7	N 1 7 / 9	6 2 / 5

Sitting: North West 3
Double Facing
Hidden Siren

Flying Star chart: Cycle 5

S		
9 8 / 4	5 4 / 9	7 6 / 2
E 8 7 / 3	1 9 / 5	**W** 3 2 / 7
4 3 / 8	**N** 6 5 / 1	2 1 / 6

Sitting: North 1
Shang Shan

S		
2 1 / 4	6 5 / 9	4 3 / 2
E 3 2 / 3	1 9 / 5	**W** 8 7 / 7
7 6 / 8	**N** 5 4 / 1	9 8 / 6

Sitting: North 2
Wang Shan

S		
2 1 / 4	6 5 / 9	4 3 / 2
E 3 2 / 3	1 9 / 5	**W** 8 7 / 7
7 6 / 8	**N** 5 4 / 1	9 8 / 6

Sitting: North 3
Wang Shan

S		
9 3 / 4	4 7 / 9	2 5 / 2
E 1 4 / 3	8 2 / 5	**W** 6 9 / 7
5 8 / 8	**N** 3 6 / 1	7 1 / 6

Sitting: North East 1
Wang Shan
Locked period eight

S		
7 1 / 4	3 6 / 9	5 8 / 2
E 6 9 / 3	8 2 / 5	**W** 1 4 / 7
2 5 / 8	**N** 4 7 / 1	9 3 / 6

Sitting: North East 2
Shang Shan
Parent String
Locked period eight

S		
7 1 / 4	3 6 / 9	5 8 / 2
E 6 9 / 3	8 2 / 5	**W** 1 4 / 7
2 5 / 8	**N** 4 7 / 1	9 3 / 6

Sitting: North East 3
Shang Shan
Parent String
Locked period eight

S		
2 6 / 4	7 2 / 9	9 4 / 2
E 1 5 / 3	3 7 / 5	**W** 5 9 / 7
6 1 / 8	**N** 8 3 / 1	4 8 / 6

Sitting: East 1
Shang Shan

S		
4 8 / 4	8 3 / 9	6 1 / 2
E 5 9 / 3	3 7 / 5	**W** 1 5 / 7
9 4 / 8	**N** 7 2 / 1	2 6 / 6

Sitting: East 2
Wang Shan

S		
4 8 / 4	8 3 / 9	6 1 / 2
E 5 9 / 3	3 7 / 5	**W** 1 5 / 7
9 4 / 8	**N** 7 2 / 1	2 6 / 6

Sitting: East 3
Wang Shan

S		
5 7 / 4	9 2 / 9	7 9 / 2
E 6 8 / 3	4 6 / 5	**W** 2 4 / 7
1 3 / 8	**N** 8 1 / 1	3 5 / 6

Sitting: South East 1
Wang Shan

S		
3 5 / 4	8 1 / 9	1 3 / 2
E 2 4 / 3	4 6 / 5	**W** 6 8 / 7
7 9 / 8	**N** 9 2 / 1	5 7 / 6

Sitting: South East 2
Shang Shan
Pearl String

S		
3 5 / 4	8 1 / 9	1 3 / 2
E 2 4 / 3	4 6 / 5	**W** 6 8 / 7
7 9 / 8	**N** 9 2 / 1	5 7 / 6

Sitting: South East 3
Shang Shan
Pearl String

Flying Star chart: Cycle 5

	S	
8 9 / 4	4 5 / 9	6 7 / 2
E 7 8 / 3	9 1 / 5	**W** 2 3 / 7
3 4 / 8	**N** 5 6 / 1	1 2 / 6

Sitting: South 1
Shang Shan

	S	
1 2 / 4	5 6 / 9	3 4 / 2
E 2 3 / 3	9 1 / 5	**W** 7 8 / 7
6 7 / 8	**N** 4 5 / 1	8 9 / 6

Sitting: South 2
Wang Shan

	S	
1 2 / 4	5 6 / 9	3 4 / 2
E 2 3 / 3	9 1 / 5	**W** 7 8 / 7
6 7 / 8	**N** 4 5 / 1	8 9 / 6

Sitting: South 3
Wang Shan

	S	
3 9 / 4	7 4 / 9	5 2 / 2
E 4 1 / 3	2 8 / 5	**W** 9 6 / 7
8 5 / 8	**N** 6 3 / 1	1 7 / 6

Sitting: South West 1
Wang Shan
Locked period eight

	S	
1 7 / 4	6 3 / 9	8 5 / 2
E 9 6 / 3	2 8 / 5	**W** 4 1 / 7
5 2 / 8	**N** 7 4 / 1	3 9 / 6

Sitting: South West 2
Shang Shan
Parent String
Locked period eight

	S	
1 7 / 4	6 3 / 9	8 5 / 2
E 9 6 / 3	2 8 / 5	**W** 4 1 / 7
5 2 / 8	**N** 7 4 / 1	3 9 / 6

Sitting: South West 3
Shang Shan
Parent String
Locked period eight

	S	
6 2 / 4	2 7 / 9	4 9 / 2
E 5 1 / 3	7 3 / 5	**W** 9 5 / 7
1 6 / 8	**N** 3 8 / 1	8 4 / 6

Sitting: West 1
Shang Shan

	S	
8 4 / 4	3 8 / 9	1 6 / 2
E 9 5 / 3	7 3 / 5	**W** 5 1 / 7
4 9 / 8	**N** 2 7 / 1	6 2 / 6

Sitting: West 2
Wang Shan

	S	
8 4 / 4	3 8 / 9	1 6 / 2
E 9 5 / 3	7 3 / 5	**W** 5 1 / 7
4 9 / 8	**N** 2 7 / 1	6 2 / 6

Sitting: West 3
Wang Shan

	S	
7 5 / 4	2 9 / 9	9 7 / 2
E 8 6 / 3	6 4 / 5	**W** 4 2 / 7
3 1 / 8	**N** 1 8 / 1	5 3 / 6

Sitting: North West 1
Wang Shan

	S	
5 3 / 4	1 8 / 9	3 1 / 2
E 4 2 / 3	6 4 / 5	**W** 8 6 / 7
9 7 / 8	**N** 2 9 / 1	7 5 / 6

Sitting: North West 2
Shang Shan
Pearl String

	S	
5 3 / 4	1 8 / 9	3 1 / 2
E 4 2 / 3	6 4 / 5	**W** 8 6 / 7
9 7 / 8	**N** 2 9 / 1	7 5 / 6

Sitting: North West 3
Shang Shan
Pearl String

Flying Star chart: Cycle 6

	S	
3 9 / 5	7 5 / 1	5 7 / 3
E 4 8 / 4	2 1 / 6	W 9 3 / 8
8 4 / 9	N 6 6 / 2	1 2 / 7

Sitting: North 1
Double Sitting

	S	
1 2 / 5	6 6 / 1	8 4 / 3
E 9 3 / 4	2 1 / 6	W 4 8 / 8
5 7 / 9	N 7 5 / 2	3 9 / 7

Sitting: North 2
Double Facing

	S	
1 2 / 5	6 6 / 1	8 4 / 3
E 9 3 / 4	2 1 / 6	W 4 8 / 8
5 7 / 9	N 7 5 / 2	3 9 / 7

Sitting: North 3
Double Facing

	S	
8 2 / 5	4 7 / 1	6 9 / 3
E 7 1 / 4	9 3 / 6	W 2 5 / 8
3 6 / 9	N 5 8 / 2	1 4 / 7

Sitting: North East 1
Shang Shan
Parent Sting

	S	
1 4 / 5	5 8 / 1	3 6 / 3
E 2 5 / 4	9 3 / 6	W 7 1 / 8
6 9 / 9	N 4 7 / 2	8 2 / 7

Sitting: North East 2
Wang Shan

	S	
1 4 / 5	5 8 / 1	3 6 / 3
E 2 5 / 4	9 3 / 6	W 7 1 / 8
6 9 / 9	N 4 7 / 2	8 2 / 7

Sitting: North East 3
Wang Shan

	S	
5 9 / 5	9 4 / 1	7 2 / 3
E 6 1 / 4	4 8 / 6	W 2 6 / 8
1 5 / 9	N 8 3 / 2	3 7 / 7

Sitting: East 1
Wang Shan
Sum to Ten
Locked period eight

	S	
3 7 / 5	8 3 / 1	1 5 / 3
E 2 6 / 4	4 8 / 6	W 6 1 / 8
7 2 / 9	N 9 4 / 2	5 9 / 7

Sitting: East 2
Shang Shan
Locked period eight

	S	
3 7 / 5	8 3 / 1	1 5 / 3
E 2 6 / 4	4 8 / 6	W 6 1 / 8
7 2 / 9	N 9 4 / 2	5 9 / 7

Sitting: East 3
Shang Shan
Locked period eight

	S	
6 6 / 5	1 2 / 1	8 4 / 3
E 7 5 / 4	5 7 / 6	W 3 9 / 8
2 1 / 9	N 9 3 / 2	4 8 / 7

Sitting: South East 1
Double Sitting
Inverse Siren

	S	
4 8 / 5	9 3 / 1	2 1 / 3
E 3 9 / 4	5 7 / 6	W 7 5 / 8
8 4 / 9	N 1 2 / 2	6 6 / 7

Sitting: South East 2
Double Facing
Hidden Siren

	S	
4 8 / 5	9 3 / 1	2 1 / 3
E 3 9 / 4	5 7 / 6	W 7 5 / 8
8 4 / 9	N 1 2 / 2	6 6 / 7

Sitting: South East 3
Double Facing
Hidden Siren

Flying Star chart: Cycle 6

	S	
9 3 5	5 7 1	7 5 3
E 8 4 4	1 2 6	**W** 3 9 8
4 8 9	**N** 6 6 2	2 1 7

Sitting: South 1
Double Facing

	S	
2 1 5	6 6 1	4 8 3
E 3 9 4	1 2 6	**W** 8 4 8
7 5 9	**N** 5 7 2	9 3 7

Sitting: South 2
Double Sitting

	S	
2 1 5	6 6 1	4 8 3
E 3 9 4	1 2 6	**W** 8 4 8
7 5 9	**N** 5 7 2	9 3 7

Sitting: South 3
Double Sitting

	S	
2 8 5	7 4 1	9 6 3
E 1 7 4	3 9 6	**W** 5 2 8
6 3 9	**N** 8 5 2	4 1 7

Sitting: South West 1
Shang Shan
Parent String

	S	
4 1 5	8 5 1	6 3 3
E 5 2 4	3 9 6	**W** 1 7 8
9 6 9	**N** 7 4 2	2 8 7

Sitting: South West 2
Wang Shan

	S	
4 1 5	8 5 1	6 3 3
E 5 2 4	3 9 6	**W** 1 7 8
9 6 9	**N** 7 4 2	2 8 7

Sitting: South West 3
Wang Shan

	S	
9 5 5	4 9 1	2 7 3
E 1 6 4	8 4 6	**W** 6 2 8
5 1 9	**N** 3 8 2	7 3 7

Sitting: West 1
Wang Shan
Sum to Ten
Locked period eight

	S	
7 3 5	3 8 1	5 1 3
E 6 2 4	8 4 6	**W** 1 6 8
2 7 9	**N** 4 9 2	9 5 7

Sitting: West 2
Shang Shan
Locked period eight

	S	
7 3 5	3 8 1	5 1 3
E 6 2 4	8 4 6	**W** 1 6 8
2 7 9	**N** 4 9 2	9 5 7

Sitting: West 3
Shang Shan
Locked period eight

	S	
6 6 5	2 1 1	4 8 3
E 5 7 4	7 5 6	**W** 9 3 8
1 2 9	**N** 3 9 2	8 4 7

Sitting: North West 1
Double Facing
Inverse Hidden

	S	
8 4 5	3 9 1	1 2 3
E 9 3 4	7 5 6	**W** 5 7 8
4 8 9	**N** 2 1 2	6 6 7

Sitting: North West 2
Double Sitting
Hidden Siren

	S	
8 4 5	3 9 1	1 2 3
E 9 3 4	7 5 6	**W** 5 7 8
4 8 9	**N** 2 1 2	6 6 7

Sitting: North West 3
Double Sitting
Hidden Siren

Flying Star chart: Cycle 7

Sitting: North 1 — Double Facing

	S	
2 3 / 6	7 7 / 2	9 5 / 4
E 1 4 / 5	3 2 / 7	W 5 9 / 9
6 8 / 1	N 8 6 / 3	4 1 / 8

Sitting: North 2 — Double Sitting — Sum to Ten

	S	
4 1 / 6	8 6 / 2	6 8 / 4
E 5 9 / 5	3 2 / 7	W 1 4 / 9
9 5 / 1	N 7 7 / 3	2 3 / 8

Sitting: North 3 — Double Sitting — Sum to Ten

	S	
4 1 / 6	8 6 / 2	6 8 / 4
E 5 9 / 5	3 2 / 7	W 1 4 / 9
9 5 / 1	N 7 7 / 3	2 3 / 8

Sitting: North East 1 — Double Facing

	S	
9 5 / 6	5 9 / 2	7 7 / 4
E 8 6 / 5	1 4 / 7	W 3 2 / 9
4 1 / 1	N 6 8 / 3	2 3 / 8

Sitting: North East 2 — Double Sitting

	S	
2 3 / 6	6 8 / 2	4 1 / 4
E 3 2 / 5	1 4 / 7	W 8 6 / 9
7 7 / 1	N 5 9 / 3	9 5 / 8

Sitting: North East 3 — Double Sitting

	S	
2 3 / 6	6 8 / 2	4 1 / 4
E 3 2 / 5	1 4 / 7	W 8 6 / 9
7 7 / 1	N 5 9 / 3	9 5 / 8

Sitting: East 1 — Shang Shan — Hidden Inverse

	S	
4 8 / 6	9 4 / 2	2 6 / 4
E 3 7 / 5	5 9 / 7	W 7 2 / 9
8 3 / 1	N 1 5 / 3	6 1 / 8

Sitting: East 2 — Wang Shan — Inverse Siren

	S	
6 1 / 6	1 5 / 2	8 3 / 4
E 7 2 / 5	5 9 / 7	W 3 7 / 9
2 6 / 1	N 9 4 / 3	4 8 / 8

Sitting: East 3 — Wang Shan — Inverse Siren

	S	
6 1 / 6	1 5 / 2	8 3 / 4
E 7 2 / 5	5 9 / 7	W 3 7 / 9
2 6 / 1	N 9 4 / 3	4 8 / 8

Sitting: South East 1 — Wang Shan — Locked in period eight

	S	
7 9 / 6	2 4 / 2	9 2 / 4
E 8 1 / 5	6 8 / 7	W 4 6 / 9
3 5 / 1	N 1 3 / 3	5 7 / 8

Sitting: South East 2 — Shang Shan — Locked in period eight — Pearl String

	S	
5 7 / 6	1 3 / 2	3 5 / 4
E 4 6 / 5	6 8 / 7	W 8 1 / 9
9 2 / 1	N 2 4 / 3	7 9 / 8

Sitting: South East 3 — Shang Shan — Locked in period eight — Pearl String

	S	
5 7 / 6	1 3 / 2	3 5 / 4
E 4 6 / 5	6 8 / 7	W 8 1 / 9
9 2 / 1	N 2 4 / 3	7 9 / 8

Flying Star chart: Cycle 7

Sitting: South 1 — Double Sitting

	S	
3 2 / 6	7 7 / 2	5 9 / 4
E 4 1 / 5	2 3 / 7	**W** 9 5 / 9
8 6 / 1	**N** 6 8 / 3	1 4 / 8

Sitting: South 2 — Double Facing — Sum to Ten

	S	
1 4 / 6	6 8 / 2	8 6 / 4
E 9 5 / 5	2 3 / 7	**W** 4 1 / 9
5 9 / 1	**N** 7 7 / 3	3 2 / 8

Sitting: South 3 — Double Facing — Sum to Ten

	S	
1 4 / 6	6 8 / 2	8 6 / 4
E 9 5 / 5	2 3 / 7	**W** 4 1 / 9
5 9 / 1	**N** 7 7 / 3	3 2 / 8

Sitting: South West 1 — Double Sitting

	S	
5 9 / 6	9 5 / 2	7 7 / 4
E 6 8 / 5	4 1 / 7	**W** 2 3 / 9
1 4 / 1	**N** 8 6 / 3	3 2 / 8

Sitting: South West 2 — Double Facing

	S	
3 2 / 6	8 6 / 2	1 4 / 4
E 2 3 / 5	4 1 / 7	**W** 6 8 / 9
7 7 / 1	**N** 9 5 / 3	5 9 / 8

Sitting: South West 3 — Double Facing

	S	
3 2 / 6	8 6 / 2	1 4 / 4
E 2 3 / 5	4 1 / 7	**W** 6 8 / 9
7 7 / 1	**N** 9 5 / 3	5 9 / 8

Sitting: West 1 — Shang Shan — Hidden Siren

	S	
8 4 / 6	4 9 / 2	6 2 / 4
E 7 3 / 5	9 5 / 7	**W** 2 7 / 9
3 8 / 1	**N** 5 1 / 3	1 6 / 8

Sitting: West 2 — Wang Shan — Inverse Siren

	S	
1 6 / 6	5 1 / 2	3 8 / 4
E 2 7 / 5	9 5 / 7	**W** 7 3 / 9
6 2 / 1	**N** 4 9 / 3	8 4 / 8

Sitting: West 3 — Wang Shan — Inverse Siren

	S	
1 6 / 6	5 1 / 2	3 8 / 4
E 2 7 / 5	9 5 / 7	**W** 7 3 / 9
6 2 / 1	**N** 4 9 / 3	8 4 / 8

Sitting: North West 1 — Wang Shan — Locked in period eight

	S	
9 7 / 6	4 2 / 2	2 9 / 4
E 1 8 / 5	8 6 / 7	**W** 6 4 / 9
5 3 / 1	**N** 3 1 / 3	7 5 / 8

Sitting: North West 2 — Shang Shan — Locked in period eight — Pearl String

	S	
7 5 / 6	3 1 / 2	5 3 / 4
E 6 4 / 5	8 6 / 7	**W** 1 8 / 9
2 9 / 1	**N** 4 2 / 3	9 7 / 8

Sitting: North West 3 — Shang Shan — Locked in period eight — Pearl String

	S	
7 5 / 6	3 1 / 2	5 3 / 4
E 6 4 / 5	8 6 / 7	**W** 1 8 / 9
2 9 / 1	**N** 4 2 / 3	9 7 / 8

Flying Star chart: Cycle 8

	S	
5 2 / 7	9 7 / 3	7 9 / 5
E 6 1 / 6	4 3 / 8	W 2 5 / 1
1 6 / 2	N 8 8 / 4	3 4 / 9

Sitting: North 1
Double Sitting

	S	
3 4 / 7	8 8 / 3	1 6 / 5
E 2 5 / 6	4 3 / 8	W 6 1 / 1
7 9 / 2	N 9 7 / 4	5 2 / 9

Sitting: North 2
Double Facing

	S	
3 4 / 7	8 8 / 3	1 6 / 5
E 2 5 / 6	4 3 / 8	W 6 1 / 1
7 9 / 2	N 9 7 / 4	5 2 / 9

Sitting: North 3
Double Facing

	S	
3 6 / 7	7 1 / 3	5 8 / 5
E 4 7 / 6	2 5 / 8	W 9 3 / 1
8 2 / 2	N 6 9 / 4	1 4 / 9

Sitting: North East 1
Wang Shan
Sum to Ten
Inverse Siren

	S	
1 4 / 7	6 9 / 3	8 2 / 5
E 9 3 / 6	2 5 / 8	W 4 7 / 1
5 8 / 2	N 7 1 / 4	3 6 / 9

Sitting: North East 2
Shang Shan
Parent String
Hidden Siren

	S	
1 4 / 7	6 9 / 3	8 2 / 5
E 9 3 / 6	2 5 / 8	W 4 7 / 1
5 8 / 2	N 7 1 / 4	3 6 / 9

Sitting: North East 3
Shang Shan
Parent String
Hidden Siren

	S	
7 9 / 7	2 5 / 3	9 7 / 5
E 8 8 / 6	6 1 / 8	W 4 3 / 1
3 4 / 2	N 1 6 / 4	5 2 / 9

Sitting: East 1
Double Sitting

	S	
5 2 / 7	1 6 / 3	3 4 / 5
E 4 3 / 6	6 1 / 8	W 8 8 / 1
9 7 / 2	N 2 5 / 4	7 9 / 9

Sitting: East 2
Double Facing

	S	
5 2 / 7	1 6 / 3	3 4 / 5
E 4 3 / 6	6 1 / 8	W 8 8 / 1
9 7 / 2	N 2 5 / 4	7 9 / 9

Sitting: East 3
Double Facing

	S	
6 8 / 7	2 4 / 3	4 6 / 5
E 5 7 / 6	7 9 / 8	W 9 2 / 1
1 3 / 2	N 3 5 / 4	8 1 / 9

Sitting: South East 1
Shang Shan
Pearl String

	S	
8 1 / 7	3 5 / 3	1 3 / 5
E 9 2 / 6	7 9 / 8	W 5 7 / 1
4 6 / 2	N 2 4 / 4	6 8 / 9

Sitting: South East 2
Wang Shan

	S	
8 1 / 7	3 5 / 3	1 3 / 5
E 9 2 / 6	7 9 / 8	W 5 7 / 1
4 6 / 2	N 2 4 / 4	6 8 / 9

Sitting: South East 3
Wang Shan

Flying Star chart: Cycle 8

	S	
2 5 / 7	7 9 / 3	9 7 / 5
E 1 6 / 6	3 4 / 8	W 5 2 / 1
6 1 / 2	N 8 8 / 4	4 3 / 9

Sitting: South 1
Double Facing

	S	
4 3 / 7	8 8 / 3	6 1 / 5
E 5 2 / 6	3 4 / 8	W 1 6 / 1
9 7 / 2	N 7 9 / 4	2 5 / 9

Sitting: South 2
Double Sitting

	S	
4 3 / 7	8 8 / 3	6 1 / 5
E 5 2 / 6	3 4 / 8	W 1 6 / 1
9 7 / 2	N 7 9 / 4	2 5 / 9

Sitting: South 3
Double Sitting

	S	
6 3 / 7	1 7 / 3	8 5 / 5
E 7 4 / 6	5 2 / 8	W 3 9 / 1
2 8 / 2	N 9 6 / 4	4 1 / 9

Sitting: South West 1
Wang Shan
Sum to Ten
Inverse Siren

	S	
4 1 / 7	9 6 / 3	2 8 / 5
E 3 9 / 6	5 2 / 8	W 7 4 / 1
8 5 / 2	N 1 7 / 4	6 3 / 9

Sitting: South West 2
Shang Shan
Parent String
Hidden Siren

	S	
4 1 / 7	9 6 / 3	2 8 / 5
E 3 9 / 6	5 2 / 8	W 7 4 / 1
8 5 / 2	N 1 7 / 4	6 3 / 9

Sitting: South West 3
Shang Shan
Parent String
Hidden Siren

	S	
9 7 / 7	5 2 / 3	7 9 / 5
E 8 8 / 6	1 6 / 8	W 3 4 / 1
4 3 / 2	N 6 1 / 4	2 5 / 9

Sitting: West 1
Double Facing

	S	
2 5 / 7	6 1 / 3	4 3 / 5
E 3 4 / 6	1 6 / 8	W 8 8 / 1
7 9 / 2	N 5 2 / 4	9 7 / 9

Sitting: West 2
Double Sitting

	S	
2 5 / 7	6 1 / 3	4 3 / 5
E 3 4 / 6	1 6 / 8	W 8 8 / 1
7 9 / 2	N 5 2 / 4	9 7 / 9

Sitting: West 3
Double Sitting

	S	
8 6 / 7	4 2 / 3	6 4 / 5
E 7 5 / 6	9 7 / 8	W 2 9 / 1
3 1 / 2	N 5 3 / 4	1 8 / 9

Sitting: North West 1
Shang Shan
Pear String

	S	
1 8 / 7	5 3 / 3	3 1 / 5
E 2 9 / 6	9 7 / 8	W 7 5 / 1
6 4 / 2	N 4 2 / 4	8 6 / 9

Sitting: North West 2
Wang Shan

	S	
1 8 / 7	5 3 / 3	3 1 / 5
E 2 9 / 6	9 7 / 8	W 7 5 / 1
6 4 / 2	N 4 2 / 4	8 6 / 9

Sitting: North West 3
Wang Shan

Flying Star chart: Cycle 9

	S	
4 5 / 8	9 9 / 4	2 7 / 6
E		W
3 6 / 7	5 4 / 9	7 2 / 2
	N	
8 1 / 3	1 8 / 5	6 3 / 1

Sitting: North 1
Double Facing
Hidden Siren

	S	
6 3 / 8	1 8 / 4	8 1 / 6
E		W
7 2 / 7	5 4 / 9	3 6 / 2
	N	
2 7 / 3	9 9 / 5	4 5 / 1

Sitting: North 2
Double Sitting
Inverse Siren

	S	
6 3 / 8	1 8 / 4	8 1 / 6
E		W
7 2 / 7	5 4 / 9	3 6 / 2
	N	
2 7 / 3	9 9 / 5	4 5 / 1

Sitting: North 3
Double Sitting
Inverse Siren

	S	
2 7 / 8	7 2 / 4	9 9 / 6
E		W
1 8 / 7	3 6 / 9	5 4 / 2
	N	
6 3 / 3	8 1 / 5	4 5 / 1

Sitting: North East 1
Double Facing

	S	
4 5 / 8	8 1 / 4	6 3 / 6
E		W
5 4 / 7	3 6 / 9	1 8 / 2
	N	
9 9 / 3	7 2 / 5	2 7 / 1

Sitting: North East 2
Double Sitting

	S	
4 5 / 8	8 1 / 4	6 3 / 6
E		W
5 4 / 7	3 6 / 9	1 8 / 2
	N	
9 9 / 3	7 2 / 5	2 7 / 1

Sitting: North East 3
Double Sitting

	S	
6 3 / 8	2 7 / 4	4 5 / 6
E		W
5 4 / 7	7 2 / 9	9 9 / 2
	N	
1 8 / 3	3 6 / 5	8 1 / 1

Sitting: East 1
Double Facing

	S	
8 1 / 8	3 6 / 4	1 8 / 6
E		W
9 9 / 7	7 2 / 9	5 4 / 2
	N	
4 5 / 3	2 7 / 5	6 3 / 1

Sitting: East 2
Double Sitting

	S	
8 1 / 8	3 6 / 4	1 8 / 6
E		W
9 9 / 7	7 2 / 9	5 4 / 2
	N	
4 5 / 3	2 7 / 5	6 3 / 1

Sitting: East 3
Double Sitting

	S	
9 9 / 8	4 5 / 4	2 7 / 6
E		W
1 8 / 7	8 1 / 9	6 3 / 2
	N	
5 4 / 3	3 6 / 5	7 2 / 1

Sitting: South East 1
Double Sitting
Locked in period eight

	S	
7 2 / 8	3 6 / 4	5 4 / 6
E		W
6 3 / 7	8 1 / 9	1 8 / 2
	N	
2 7 / 3	4 5 / 5	9 9 / 1

Sitting: South East 2
Double Facing
Sum to Ten
Locked in period eight

	S	
7 2 / 8	3 6 / 4	5 4 / 6
E		W
6 3 / 7	8 1 / 9	1 8 / 2
	N	
2 7 / 3	4 5 / 5	9 9 / 1

Sitting: South East 3
Double Facing
Sum to Ten
Locked in period eight

Flying Star chart: Cycle 9

Sitting: South 1

	S	
5 4 8	9 9 4	7 2 6
E 6 3 7	4 5 9	**W** 2 7 2
1 8 3	**N** 8 1 5	3 6 1

Sitting: South 1
Double Sitting
Hidden Siren

Sitting: South 2

	S	
3 6 8	8 1 4	1 8 6
E 2 7 7	4 5 9	**W** 6 3 2
7 2 3	**N** 9 9 5	5 4 1

Sitting: South 2
Double Facing
Inverse Siren

Sitting: South 3

	S	
3 6 8	8 1 4	1 8 6
E 2 7 7	4 5 9	**W** 6 3 2
7 2 3	**N** 9 9 5	5 4 1

Sitting: South 3
Double Facing
Inverse Siren

Sitting: South West 1

	S	
7 2 8	2 7 4	9 9 6
E 8 1 7	6 3 9	**W** 4 5 2
3 6 3	1 8 5	5 4 1

Sitting: South West 1
Double Sitting

Sitting: South West 2

	S	
5 4 8	1 8 4	3 6 6
E 4 5 7	6 3 9	**W** 8 1 2
9 9 3	2 7 5	7 2 1

Sitting: South West 2
Double Facing

Sitting: South West 3

	S	
5 4 8	1 8 4	3 6 6
E 4 5 7	6 3 9	**W** 8 1 2
9 9 3	2 7 5	7 2 1

Sitting: South West 3
Double Facing

Sitting: West 1

	S	
3 6 8	7 2 4	5 4 6
E 4 5 7	2 7 9	**W** 9 9 2
8 1 3	6 3 5	1 8 1

Sitting: West 1
Double Sitting

Sitting: West 2

	S	
1 8 8	6 3 4	8 1 6
E 9 9 7	2 7 9	**W** 4 5 2
5 4 3	7 2 5	3 6 1

Sitting: West 2
Double Facing

Sitting: West 3

	S	
1 8 8	6 3 4	8 1 6
E 9 9 7	2 7 9	**W** 4 5 2
5 4 3	7 2 5	3 6 1

Sitting: West 3
Double Facing

Sitting: North West 1

	S	
9 9 8	5 4 4	7 2 6
E 8 1 7	1 8 9	**W** 3 6 2
4 5 3	**N** 6 3 5	2 7 1

Sitting: North West 1
Double Facing
Locked in period eight

Sitting: North West 2

	S	
2 7 8	6 3 4	4 5 6
E 3 6 7	1 8 9	**W** 8 1 2
7 2 3	**N** 5 4 5	9 9 1

Sitting: North West 2
Double Sitting
Sum to Ten
Locked in period eight

Sitting: North West 3

	S	
2 7 8	6 3 4	4 5 6
E 3 6 7	1 8 9	**W** 8 1 2
7 2 3	**N** 5 4 5	9 9 1

Sitting: North West 3
Double Sitting
Sum to Ten
Locked in period eight

**If you enjoyed *Flying Star Feng Shui Made Easy*,
check out this iUniverse title:**

D.E. Tarver
The Art of War

Sun Tzu and Sun Pin's timeless strategic masterpieces are constantly analyzed and interpreted by leaders worldwide. For the first time ever, author D.E. Tarver explains the classic texts *The Art of War* by Sun Tzu and *The Art of Warfare* by Sun Pin in plain English.

War is the perfect training ground for teaching Sun Tzu's ancient philosophies to attaining victory over an opponent. **The Art of War** outlines the steps for outwitting the enemy, be it an army of 10,000 or an unresponsive client.

The Art of War teaches leaders strategies to attain victory by:
· Knowing when to stand up to an opponent, and when to back down.
· How to be confident without being overly confident.
· Considering the cost of the campaign before launching an attack.
· Avoiding an opponent's strengths and striking his weaknesses.

"The one who is first to the field of battle has time to rest, while his opponent rushes into the conflict weary and confused. The first will be fresh and alert. The second will waste most of his energy trying to catch up." Be the first to the battlefield with **The Art of War**.

**Available through your local bookstore
or at www.iuniverse.com.**

 iUniverse™
Star

0-595-09966-1